Battleg

BRUNEVAL

ON WILKINSON

Battleground series:

Stamford Bridge & Hastings *by* Peter Marren
Wars of the Roses - **Wakefield / Towton** *by* Philip A. Haigh
Wars of the Roses - **Barnet** *by* David Clark
Wars of the Roses - **Tewkesbury** *by* Steven Goodchild
Wars of the Roses - **The Battles of St Albans** *by* Peter Burley, Michael Elliott & Harvey Wilson
English Civil War - **Naseby** *by* Martin Marix Evans, Peter Burton and Michael Westaway
English Civil War - **Marston Moor** *by* David Clark
War of the Spanish Succession - **Blenheim 1704** *by* James Falkner
War of the Spanish Succession - **Ramillies 1706** *by* James Falkner
Napoleonic - **Hougoumont** *by* Julian Paget and Derek Saunders
Napoleonic - **Waterloo** *by* Andrew Uffindell and Michael Corum
Zulu War - **Isandlwana** *by* Ian Knight and Ian Castle
Zulu War - **Rorkes Drift** *by* Ian Knight and Ian Castle
Boer War - **The Relief of Ladysmith** *by* Lewis Childs
Boer War - **The Siege of Ladysmith** *by* Lewis Childs
Boer War - **Kimberley** *by* Lewis Childs

Mons *by* Jack Horsfall and Nigel Cave
Néry *by* Patrick Tackle
Le Cateau *by* Nigel Cave and Jack Shelden
Walking the Salient *by* Paul Reed
Ypres - **Sanctuary Wood and Hooge** *by* Nigel Cave
Ypres - **Hill 60** *by* Nigel Cave
Ypres - **Messines Ridge** *by* Peter Oldham
Ypres - **Polygon Wood** *by* Nigel Cave
Ypres - **Passchendaele** *by* Nigel Cave
Ypres - **Airfields and Airmen** *by* Mike O'Connor
Ypres - **St Julien** *by* Graham Keech
Ypres - **Boesinghe** *by* Stephen McGreal
Walking the Somme *by* Paul Reed
Somme - **Gommecourt** *by* Nigel Cave
Somme - **Serre** *by* Jack Horsfall & Nigel Cave
Somme - **Beaumont Hamel** *by* Nigel Cave
Somme - **Thiepval** *by* Michael Stedman
Somme - **La Boisselle** *by* Michael Stedman
Somme - **Fricourt** *by* Michael Stedman
Somme - **Carnoy-Montauban** *by* Graham Maddocks
Somme - **Pozières** *by* Graham Keech
Somme - **Courcelette** *by* Paul Reed
Somme - **Boom Ravine** *by* Trevor Pidgeon
Somme - **Mametz Wood** *by* Michael Renshaw
Somme - **Delville Wood** *by* Nigel Cave
Somme - **Advance to Victory (North) 1918** *by* Michael Stedman
Somme - **Flers** *by* Trevor Pidgeon
Somme - **Bazentin Ridge** *by* Edward Hancock
Somme - **Combles** *by* Paul Reed
Somme - **Beaucourt** *by* Michael Renshaw
Somme - **Redan Ridge** *by* Michael Renshaw
Somme - **Hamel** *by* Peter Pedersen
Somme - **Villers-Bretonneux** *by* Peter Pedersen
Somme - **Airfields and Airmen** *by* Mike O'Connor
Airfields and Airmen of the Channel Coast *by* Mike O'Connor
In the Footsteps of the Red Baron *by* Mike O'Connor
Arras - **Airfields and Airmen** *by* Mike O'Connor
Arras - **The Battle for Vimy Ridge** *by* Jack Sheldon & Nigel Cave
Arras - **Vimy Ridge** *by* Nigel Cave
Arras - **Gavrelle** *by* Trevor Tasker and Kyle Tallett
Arras - **Oppy Wood** *by* David Bilton
Arras - **Bullecourt** *by* Graham Keech
Arras - **Monchy le Preux** *by* Colin Fox
Walking Arras *by* Paul Reed
Hindenburg Line *by* Peter Oldham
Hindenburg Line - **Epehy** *by* Bill Mitchinson
Hindenburg Line - **Riqueval** *by* Bill Mitchinson
Hindenburg Line - **Villers-Plouich** *by* Bill Mitchinson
Hindenburg Line - **Cambrai Right Hook** *by* Jack Horsfall & Nigel Cave
Hindenburg Line - **Cambrai Flesquières** *by* Jack Horsfall & Nigel Cave
Hindenburg Line - **Saint Quentin** *by* Helen McPhail and Philip Guest
Hindenburg Line - **Bourlon Wood** *by* Jack Horsfall & Nigel Cave
Cambrai - **Airfields and Airmen** *by* Mike O'Connor
Aubers Ridge *by* Edward Hancock

La Bassée - **Neuve Chapelle** *by* Geoffrey Bridger
Loos - **Hohenzollern Redoubt** *by* Andrew Rawson
Loos - **Hill 70** *by* Andrew Rawson
Fromelles *by* Peter Pedersen
The Battle of the Lys 1918 *by* Phil Tomaselli
Accrington Pals Trail *by* William Turner
Poets at War: Wilfred Owen *by* Helen McPhail and Philip Guest
Poets at War: Edmund Blunden *by* Helen McPhail and Philip Guest
Poets at War: Graves & Sassoon *by* Helen McPhail and Philip Guest
Gallipoli *by* Nigel Steel
Gallipoli - **Gully Ravine** *by* Stephen Chambers
Gallipoli - **Anzac Landing** *by* Stephen Chambers
Gallipoli - **Suvla August Offensive** *by* Stephen Chambers
Gallipoli - **Landings at Helles** *by* Huw & Jill Rodge
Walking the Italian Front *by* Francis Mackay
Italy - **Asiago** *by* Francis Mackay
Verdun: **Fort Douamont** *by* Christina Holstein
Verdun: **Fort Vaux** *by* Christina Holstein
Walking Verdun *by* Christina Holstein
Zeebrugge & Ostend Raids 1918 *by* Stephen McGreal

Germans at Beaumont Hamel *by* Jack Sheldon
Germans at Thiepval *by* Jack Sheldon

SECOND WORLD WAR

Dunkirk *by* Patrick Wilson
Calais *by* Jon Cooksey
Boulogne *by* Jon Cooksey
Saint-Nazaire *by* James Dorrian
Walking D-Day *by* Paul Reed
Atlantic Wall - **Pas de Calais** *by* Paul Williams
Atlantic Wall - **Normandy** *by* Paul Williams
Normandy - **Pegasus Bridge** *by* Carl Shilleto
Normandy - **Merville Battery** *by* Carl Shilleto
Normandy - **Utah Beach** *by* Carl Shilleto
Normandy - **Omaha Beach** *by* Tim Kilvert-Jones
Normandy - **Gold Beach** *by* Christopher Dunphie & Garry Johnson
Normandy - **Gold Beach Jig** *by* Tim Saunders
Normandy - **Juno Beach** *by* Tim Saunders
Normandy - **Sword Beach** *by* Tim Kilvert-Jones
Normandy - **Operation Bluecoat** *by* Ian Daglish
Normandy - **Operation Goodwood** *by* Ian Daglish
Normandy - **Epsom** *by* Tim Saunders
Normandy - **Hill 112** *by* Tim Saunders
Normandy - **Mont Pinçon** *by* Eric Hunt
Normandy - **Cherbourg** *by* Andrew Rawson
Normandy - **Commandos & Rangers on D-Day** *by* Tim Saunders
Das Reich – **Drive to Normandy** *by* Philip Vickers
Oradour *by* Philip Beck
Market Garden - **Nijmegen** *by* Tim Saunders
Market Garden - **Hell's Highway** *by* Tim Saunders
Market Garden - **Arnhem, Oosterbeek** *by* Frank Steer
Market Garden - **Arnhem, The Bridge** *by* Frank Steer
Market Garden - **The Island** *by* Tim Saunders
Rhine Crossing – **US 9th Army & 17th US Airborne** *by* Andrew Raw
British Rhine Crossing – **Operation Varsity** *by* Tim Saunders
British Rhine Crossing – **Operation Plunder** *by* Tim Saunders
Battle of the Bulge – **St Vith** *by* Michael Tolhurst
Battle of the Bulge – **Bastogne** *by* Michael Tolhurst
Channel Islands *by* George Forty
Walcheren *by* Andrew Rawson
Remagen Bridge *by* Andrew Rawson
Cassino *by* Ian Blackwell
Anzio *by* Ian Blackwell
Dieppe *by* Tim Saunders
Fort Eben Emael *by* Tim Saunders
Crete – **The Airborne Invasion** *by* Tim Saunders
Malta *by* Paul Williams
Bruneval Raid *by* Paul Oldfield
Cockleshell Raid *by* Paul Oldfield

Battleground Europe

BRUNEVAL

PAUL OLDFIELD

Pen & Sword
MILITARY

First published in Great Britain in 2013 by
Pen & Sword Military
an imprint of
Pen & Sword Books Ltd
47 Church Street
Barnsley
South Yorkshire
S70 2AS

ISBN 9781781590676

A CIP catalogue record for this book is available from the British Library

Typeset in 10 pt Palatino by
Factionpress
Printed and bound by CPI Group (UK) Ltd, Croydon, CR0 4YY

Pen & Sword Books Ltd incorporates the Imprints of Pen & Sword Aviation, Pen & Sword Maritime, Pen & Sword Military, Wharncliffe Local History, Pen and Sword Select, Pen and Sword Military Classics, Leo Cooper, Remember When, Seaforth Publishing and Frontline Publishing, Claymore Press.
For a complete list of Pen & Sword titles please contact
PEN & SWORD BOOKS LIMITED
47 Church Street, Barnsley, South Yorkshire, S70 2AS, England
E-mail: enquiries@pen-and-sword.co.uk
Website: www.pen-and-sword.co.uk

CONTENTS

Introduction

THE BRUNEVAL RAID is unique. In the year of the great raids, 1942, it stands alone as the only one launched purely to satisfy the needs of scientific intelligence. It was also one of the first fully combined operations put together by HQ Combined Operations under Mountbatten. The results were out of all proportion to the resources committed.

This book covers the development of radar, the search for German radar in the Second World War, the discovery of *Würzburg* radar at Bruneval, the planning and preparations for the audacious raid, its highly successful execution and the aftermath. There is a wealth of colourful characters involved, from world-class scientists, outstanding reconnaissance pilots, Resistance agents, famous sailors, soldiers and airmen, an escaped German Jew and, most importantly, not forgetting the vast majority of the ordinary people involved doing extraordinary things to win the war. We will also meet a number of those on the other side of the hill; all fascinating characters, many destined to be future allies in NATO.

Research involved consulting numerous sources and there is a list at the end, which readers may find useful for further study of their own. However, this book does cover the issues and events comprehensively. I would commend particularly the files in the National Archives and those people in the past with the foresight to retain the documents within them. These enabled me to unravel a number of issues that seemed never to have been satisfactorily resolved, such as who dropped the two and a half sticks of paratroopers in the wrong place and the sequence by which the evacuation beach was stormed and by whom. I would like to thank Jon Baker, Rebecca Skinner, Bob Hilton and Joe Hamon who, at short notice, found key documents to identify who took part in the raid and provided some photographs from the Airborne Forces Museum archives.

However, there is one important issue that remains a mystery – what happened to the *Würzburg* components brought back from Bruneval? I would be delighted to hear from anyone who can throw light on where these historically unique and important items are now, as they warrant being displayed somewhere publically and prominently.

Paul Oldfield
Wiltshire
January 2012

Chapter One

DEVELOPMENT OF RADAR

DURING the Second World War the British referred to what would later be universally known as radar, as Radio Direction Finding (RDF). The Germans called it *Dezimeter Telegraphie* (DT). Radar, an American term (radio direction and ranging), will be used throughout for the sake of simplicity and consistency.

In the late 19th Century, Heinrich Hertz demonstrated that metal sheets reflected radio waves. By 1904 Christian Hulsmeyer had patented a transmitter/receiver for ships to detect other ships; it was well ahead of its time. Three developments in the 1920s allowed for the later development of radar. In 1924, Americans Gregory Briet and Merle A Tuve sent out radio waves in pulses. In 1927, Dr Hans Hollmann, of the Technical University in Darmstadt, built the first ultra short wave transmitter/receiver for centimeter and decimeter waves. In 1929, Hidetsugu Yagi published work on directional antennas in Japan, which made narrow beam signals possible.

In 1931, a pulsed radio system was fitted to the French liner *Normandie* to detect icebergs and ships. In 1933 Rudolf Kuhnold, Chief of the German Navy Signals Research Department detected a battleship at 500 metres in Kiel harbour. By October 1934 he had extended the range to 11 kilometres (kms). When demonstrated to the head of the Navy, Grand Admiral Erich Raeder, in September 1935, the audience was stunned. By using pulses rather than continuous waves, Kuhnold extended the range to 19 kms the next year.

In Germany two electronics companies, GEMA and Telefunken, took forward the development of radar. By 1936 GEMA had produced the *Freya* early warning radar with a range of 50 kms, increased later to 120 kms. The same year Telefunken produced the *Würzburg* radar, which complemented Freya; it was more accurate, but had a range of only 10 kms. In 1937 *Würzburg's* range was increased to 35 kms. GEMA also produced the *Seetakt* gun ranging radar, which was fitted to *Graf Spee*. So by the start of the Second World War the Germans had made considerable advances in radar technology and had capable equipment in service. None of this was known across the Channel in Britain, where radar had been developed in isolation to advances in Germany.

On 10 November 1932, Prime Minister Stanley Baldwin told Parliament that the bomber would always get through and air exercises over the following summers supported his assertion.

Freya FuMG 39G radar produced by Gesellschaft fur Elektroakustische und Mechanische Apparate (GEMA).

Telefunken developed the Würzburg radar.

German pocket-battleship *Graf Spee.*

Senior officials in the Air Ministry began to question whether Britain was able to withstand air attack; defences were virtually non-existent. Sound locators and acoustic mirrors for early warning proved inadequate; a demonstration of a sound locator at Biggin Hill was drowned out by a passing milk cart! Work on infrared detection by Dr R V Jones at the Clarendon Laboratory, Oxford also proved to be ineffective.

It was clear to many that war was coming and something had to be done. In June 1934, A P Rowe, Personal Assistant to H E Wimperis, Director of Scientific Research at the Air Ministry, warned that

Experimental acoustic mirrors were constructed around the coast. In still air they could detect aircraft 15 miles away, allowing only a few minutes warning. They were unable to ascertain speed and altitude and only a few were capable of working out in which direction the aircraft was moving.

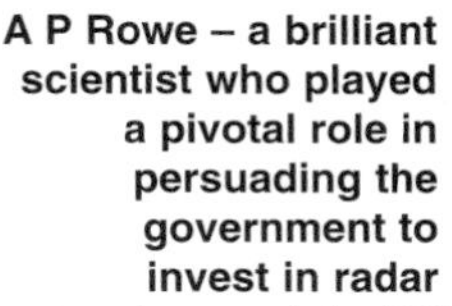

Dr (later Professor) R V Jones, whose work at Oxford ruled out using infrared to detect aircraft, was later instrumental in the genesis of the Bruneval Raid.

A P Rowe – a brilliant scientist who played a pivotal role in persuading the government to invest in radar development. In 1935 he coined the acronym RDF as a cover for the research work. During the war, as Chief Superintendent of the Telecommunications Research Establishment, he held regular informal meetings with his staff and senior scientific and military officials from London, known as Sunday Soviets. Everyone, regardless of seniority was encouraged to contribute ideas and those of merit could be adopted immediately because the main decision-makers were there.

H E Wimperis, Director of Scientific Research at the Air Ministry, who first proposed the Committee for the Scientific Survey of Air Defence

A Sunday Soviet at Malvern later in the war. A P Rowe sits slightly left of centre behind the desk. Lord Cherwell, Churchill's scientific adviser sits in the armchair in front of the fireplace.

unless science evolved new methods of aiding defence, Britain was likely to lose the next war. That November, Wimperis proposed setting up the Committee for the Scientific Survey of Air Defence. Secretary of State for Air, Lord Londonderry, agreed to its formation to investigate air defence with the utmost urgency. It became known as the Tizard Committee after its Chairman, Sir Henry Tizard; Rowe was Secretary.

Sir Henry Tizard – a chemist and mathematician who was Rector of Imperial College London 1929-42. In 1933 he became Chairman of the Aeronautical Research Committee and was a champion of the development of radar. He resigned following a meeting with Churchill in 1940, during which R V Jones demonstrated that Tizard's views on German radio-beam bombing aids were incorrect. He then led the Tizard Mission, which passed on to the Americans many key advances in radar, jet engine and nuclear technology.

Robert Watson-Watt, Superintendent of the Radio Research Unit at Slough, was asked to research the feasibility of a beam weapon to damage enemy aircraft. The energy required was unachievable at the time and the idea was shelved. However, Watson-Watt believed it was possible to detect aircraft by sending out radio pulses and receiving the reflected echoes, if special transmitters and receivers were developed. Accordingly the first meeting of the Tizard Committee on 28 January 1935 asked Watson-Watt to report on the viability of radio detection of aircraft.

As early as 1923, HM Signal School had noted signals being disturbed by the passage of aircraft. In 1931, General Post Office experiments at Dollis Hill on VHF radios to link the Hebrides, also noticed that passing aircraft produced a flutter in the headphones. Watson-Watt, assisted by A F Wilkins, worked out the power required and realised it was a feasible method for detecting aircraft. On 14 February, Watson-Watt presented his paper, 'The Detection and Location of Aircraft by Radio Methods to the Tizard Committee.

The paper proved to be a breakthrough and the pace quickened. Next day Wimperis presented the Committee's recommendation to the man in charge of RAF research and development and destined to be the first Commander-in-Chief of Fighter Command, Air Marshal Sir Hugh Dowding. He allocated £10,000 immediately, pending a practical demonstration.

Sir Robert Alexander Watson-Watt – descended from James Watt, the famous steam engineer. He ruled out the feasibility of beam weapons, but believed aircraft could be detected by reflected radio pulses and is considered by many to be the father of British radar. Later in life he was caught speeding in Canada by a radar-gun and told the policeman, 'Had I known what you were going to do with it I would never have invented it!' He penned an ironic poem, 'Rough Justice':

Pity Sir Robert Watson-Watt,
Strange target of this radar plot
And thus, with others I can mention,
The victim of his own invention.
His magical all-seeing eye
Enabled cloud-bound planes to fly
But now by some ironic twist
It spots the speeding motorist
And bites, no doubt with legal wit,
The hand that once created it.

A F Wilkins – set up the Daventry experiment in February 1935 that led to the development of British radar.

Air Marshal Sir Hugh Dowding – he became Member for Supply and Research on the Air Council in 1930. He saw the days of the biplane were numbered and pushed for fast all metal fighters like the Hurricane and Spitfire. He also had the foresight to allocate funds to develop radar

The Morris van with Eccles ambulance body used as a mobile laboratory for the Daventry experiment. The actual apparatus used by Wilkins is in the Science Museum.

A sketch made by A F Wilkins of the layout for the Daventry experiment.

Handley Page Heyford bomber.

BIRTH OF RADAR MEMORIAL
ON 26th FEBRUARY 1935 IN THE FIELD OPPOS
ROBERT WATSON WATT AND
ARNOLD WILKINS
SHOWED FOR THE FIRST TIME IN BRITAIN THA
AIRCRAFT COULD BE DETECTED BY BOUNCIN
RADIO WAVES OFF THEM. BY 1939 THERE WE
20 STATIONS TRACKING AIRCRAFT AT DISTANC
UP TO MORE THAN 100 MILES. LATER KNOW
AS RADAR. IT WAS THIS INVENTION MORE
THAN ANY OTHER THAT SAVED THE RAF
FROM DEFEAT IN THE 1940 BATTLE OF BRITAI

Memorial on the site where A F Wilkins, Robert Watson-Watt and A P Rowe carried out the first detection experiment near Weedon on 26 February 1935.

Wilkins installed a modified short-wave receiver in a Morris KX50 van fitted with an Eccles ambulance body and parked it in a field just off the A5 near the old Army School of Equitation at Weedon. On 26 February 1935 he, Watson-Watt and A P Rowe waited for a Handley Page Heyford bomber from the Royal Aircraft Establishment Farnborough to fly through the BBC shortwave transmissions from Borough Hill near Daventry. The signal was steady until the bomber flew through it, then the line on the oscilloscope bent; it had been detected 13 kms away. Wilkins later said, 'It was clear to all who watched the tube on that occasion that we were at the beginning of great developments in the art of air defence'. Rowe dashed back to London and extra research money was allocated immediately.

The Radio Research Unit at Slough moved to a former First World War weapons testing site at Orford Ness, Suffolk in May 1935. Towers were erected for the first experiments and by July the detection range had been improved to 64 kms. The land-based radar system developed there by Watson Watt's team became known as Chain Home. Progress was such that in December the Treasury authorized construction of the first five stations to cover the eastern approaches to London; these included the stations at Bawdsey, Dunkirk in Kent and Swingate near Dover.

The Unit quickly outgrew Orford Ness and a nearby airfield complained about the height of the towers, which had grown to 73 metres. Rowe persuaded the Treasury to purchase Bawdsey Manor, about 20 kms away, and the Unit moved there in February 1936. By March a single aircraft could be tracked at 130 kms and in September, Bawdsey took part in the first RAF air exercises using radar. By May 1937 radar was thought to be capable of real operations. The Tizard Committee asked for the money to develop a nationwide operational system and got it.

Bawdsey Manor with experimental radar masts.

It was planned to have twenty stations, each with 106 metre steel transmitter towers and 73 metre wooden receiver towers

Location of the first 20 Chain Home stations built before war broke out and the high level coverage (4,600 metres) achieved by September 1939. During the war extra stations were added to fill in gaps and extend the system westwards. Chain Home Low stations were also added to detect enemy aircraft flying in at low level.

They were able to give range, direction and altitude at 190 kms and were accurate to about three miles, which was close enough for a fighter to spot its target in daylight. However, it became clear that if the remaining fifteen stations were not started until the first batch of five was complete, it would be the spring of 1940 before the system was ready. The Air Ministry and Treasury had the foresight to go ahead with the whole project to ensure they were ready by 1938. By the outbreak of war, Britain was effectively surrounded by a 19 kms high and 190 kms thick electronic wall.

Although radar was vital for air defence, it was not the complete answer. Techniques for directing fighters, communicating by radio and keeping track of enemy and friendly aircraft were needed, all of which had to be integrated with searchlights, barrage balloons, anti-aircraft artillery and ground observers. Air interception exercises (the Biggin Hill experiments) began in February 1936, before radar was ready. These experiments resulted in the world's first integrated air defence system being in place when war broke out in September 1939 and enabled the Battle of Britain to be won.

Chain Home signals were relatively long-wave, which required large antennas and supporting towers that could not fail to come to the attention of the Germans. In 1937-38 unarmed He 111s overflew Britain on behalf of *Lufthansa* to carry out timetable and weather checks. In reality these were

Chain Home station at Swingate, Dover – the 360' high transmitter towers on the left were made of steel (two are still there) – the 240' high wooden receiver towers are on the right.

***Lufthansa* Heinkel civil aircraft were flown over Britain's on photographic reconnaissance flights in 1937-38.**

photographic reconnaissance flights for the Air Ministry in Berlin. Chain Home stations were included, but priority went to dockyards, RAF stations and aircraft factories. General Wolfgang Martini, commanding *Luftwaffe* Signals, didn't believe the towers were part of a radar system, but had them checked out anyway. He loaded the dirigible *Graf Zeppelin* with receivers in May 1939 and flew it from Friedrichshafen across the North Sea towards Bawdsey. It was tracked moving along the coast in thick weather and it amused Fighter Command HQ when its reported position was nine miles out. *Graf Zeppelin* made three separate flights up to August and failed to pick up the radar signals. *Abwehr* agents, the German Air Attaché and visiting *Luftwaffe* generals Milch and Udet also failed to pick up anything about radar. However, the converse was also true, as the British knew little or nothing about German radar development.

***Graf Zeppelin* photographed during a reconnaissance flight in July 1939.**

When war broke out the Bawdsey team moved to Dundee, which was safer, but totally unsuitable for its work. In May 1940 it moved to Worth Matravers near Swanage in Dorset and naming it the Telecommunications Research Establishment (TRE Worth) masked its secret purpose. Early work there created thirty Chain Home Low stations to detect aircraft flying under

Telecommunications Research Establishment at Worth Matravers in Dorset in 1940.

Chain Home radar coverage. Air interception radar was developed there for night fighters. The first experiments detected a bicycle being ridden up and down a track on top of the cliffs at St Aldhelm's Head. This development also led to airborne radar capable of detecting surfaced U-boats. By August 1940, TRE had radar capable of detecting individual buildings, the first being the chapel at St Aldhelm's Head. This developed into H2S airborne ground scanning radar, which allowed RAF Bomber Command to bomb through heavy cloud. TRE also developed radar jammers and Window (chaff) amongst many other devices.

A bicycle ridden along this track was the first object detected by experimental air interception radar. In the distance is the chapel at St Aldhelm's Head, the first building detected by ground scanning radar.

Chapter Two

GENESIS OF THE RAID

IN 1939, DR R V JONES was appointed Britain's first Scientific Intelligence Officer at the Air Ministry. Early in the war much of his time was spent helping to win the 'battle of the beams', (See Appendix I) as scientists on both sides struggled for advantage in the aerial bombing war. Jones also spent the first years of the conflict convincing doubters the Germans actually had radar, researching how advanced they were in radar technology and persuading senior officials that it was responsible for increasing bomber losses. On 12 June 1940, Professor Frederick Lindemann, Churchill's scientific adviser, asked Jones if he believed the Germans had radar. Jones did and gave him the evidence he had – prisoner interrogation reports, the Oslo Report and the *Graf Spee*:

> In May 1940 a German prisoner had mentioned a radio gun laying and ranging device used by the Navy; this was the *Seetakt* radar system. Other prisoners mentioned a *Luftwaffe* radio warning system.
>
> In November 1939 the British Naval Attaché in Oslo, Captain Hector Boyes, was delivered an anonymous report covering the German application of science to war, including radio detection. A copy of the report reached Jones via Group Captain Fred Winterbotham, head of the Air Section at Military Intelligence 6 (MI6). At the time many believed the Oslo Report was a plant.

Professor Frederick Alexander Lindemann

Influential physicist and scientific adviser to Churchill; known as "the Prof". The son of a naturalized German father and American mother, educated in Berlin and at the Sorbonne. An accomplished pianist and tennis player; he competed at Wimbledon. Being teetotal, a non-smoker and a vegetarian, he was the very opposite of Churchill. Lindemann was not always correct; he advocated aerial mines and infrared beams ahead of radar and did much to disrupt the work of the Tizard Committee. Later in the war he argued against evidence of V2 rocket development. He was made Baron in 1941 and Viscount in 1956. After the war he returned to the Clarendon at Oxford, but also held political office as Paymaster-General and created the Atomic Energy Authority

Taken at Montevideo shortly before *Graf Spee* was scuttled. The *Seetakt* gun ranging radar antenna is the rectangular device circled, close to the top of the mast.

Jones didn't and, when he had a rare quiet moment as the war progressed, he flicked through it to see what was likely to be coming next; he was rarely disappointed. The author was Hans Ferdinand Mayer, director of the Siemens research laboratory in Berlin. Jones met Mayer in the 1950s, but in accordance with his wishes, did not reveal his identity until Mayer and his wife died in the 1980s.

Hans Ferdinand Ma German physicist a mathematician. He signed the Oslo Re 'a German scientist who is on your side 1943 he was arreste for listening to BBC radio transmissions criticising the Nazis spent the rest of th war in concentratio camps. He worked i America post-war, returning to Germa 1950 to head the Siemens & Halske research departme

Seetakt radar was developed by the Germans for gunnery control. An unusual antenna array had been spotted on *Graf Spee* before the war and reported to the Admiralty. When *Graf Spee* was scuttled in the River Plate in December 1939, a British radar specialist, L Bainbridge Bell, climbed aboard her and examined the antenna. He concluded it may be part of a ranging radar, but he was not conclusive and the report was shelved.

Following Lindemann's meeting with Jones, more evidence became available. On 5 July an intelligence source learned that German fighters had intercepted some aircraft due to the excellence of '*Freya-Meldung*' (Freya reporting). Then, on 14 July, mention was made of *Freya Gerät* (device). Jones concluded Freya was associated

Group Captain Frederick William Winterbotham

A First World War pilot taken prisoner in 1917. He spent time in Germany in the 1930s working for MI6, even meeting Hitler and other senior Nazis. During the war, Winterbotham distributed a great deal of Ultra intelligence under the auspices of MI6 to protect the source at Bletchley Park. In 1974 he published The Ultra Secret, the first book to explain fully what Ultra was about.

with air defence and asked for any reports that mentioned it. In mythology he read the goddess Freya had slept with four dwarves in order to possess Brisingamen, a wonderful necklace. Loki stole it from her while she slept, but was seen by Heimdal, who could see 100 miles day and night. Heimdal recovered Brisingamen and returned it to Freya. Could the Germans really be so obvious?

Intelligence learned of a heavily guarded *Freya* station at Lannion on the north coast of Cotes-du-Nord department in Brittany, but air reconnaissance showed nothing unusual. The British radar system, Chain Home, used enormous towers and nothing of the kind could be found along the French coast, so Jones concluded the Germans had to be using a different system.

On 29 July the destroyer HMS *Delight*, was attacked by sixteen enemy aircraft 95 kms off the French coast, having done nothing to reveal her position. There was a major fire and an explosion and she sank in Portland harbour that evening, with the loss of six of her company. This attack was either an incredible coincidence or the ship had been detected by some form of radar. Soon after another intelligence report identified a *Freya* station on Cap de la Hague, northwest of the port of Cherbourg. Given its loc-

Key sites identified by British intelligence in the hunt for German radar. X marks the position where HMS *Delight* was attacked on 29 July 1940.

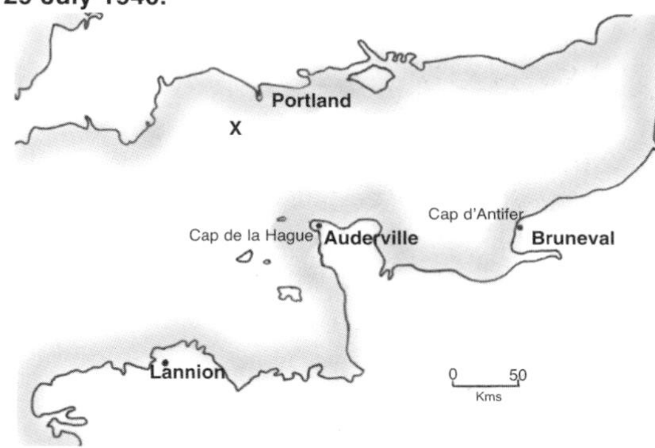

HMS *Delight* entered service in 1933 and served in the Mediterranean, Persian Gulf, China Station and Red Sea during the 1935 Abyssinian crisis. She transferred to the Home Fleet in December 1939 and was involved in the Norwegian campaign. She lies in 60 metres of water broken into several sections.

Leading Seaman Cyril H Ralph Day from Lymington in Hampshire, died on 29th July 1940, a victim of the bombing of HMS Delight. He is buried in Portland Royal Naval Cemetery.

ation, Jones believed it might have been responsible for detecting HMS *Delight*.

Unidentified wireless signals were picked up from across the Channel. In November 1940, Derrick Garrard was attached to Jones' staff at the Air Ministry, having previously worked on radar at TRE Worth. He packed receiving equipment into his car and drove east along the Downs listening. Near Dover he picked up signals around 375 Megahertz (MHz). Although unknown at the time these were from *Seetakt* radars used by German batteries to direct long-range guns onto British shipping in the Channel. Garrard also picked up transmissions around 120 MHz and took bearings on their origin. His work would prove hugely significant later; for his troubles he was arrested for suspicious activity.

With more and more evidence stacking up that the Germans had a sophisticated radar capability, Jones asked for detailed photographic reconnaissance coverage of Cap de la Hague. In January 1941 according to Jones (22 November 1940 in some accounts and February in others), he was shown pictures of enclosures about six metres across west of Auderville on Cap de la Hague. When Dr Charles Frank checked them with a stereoscope, he saw from the shadows that between exposures a structure had rotated slightly. Could it be a radar antenna? Low oblique dicing missions (so called because the pilots were dicing with death) were delayed because the priority for the Photographic Reconnaissance Unit

Frederick Charles Frank - was at the Chemical Defence Experimental Station at Porton Down in Wiltshire until 1940 when he transferred to the Air Ministry's Directorate of Intelligence (Science) to work with RV Jones. Post-war at the University of Bristol, he researched solid-state physics and crystal dislocation. He was knighted in 1977.

The two photographs examined by Charles Frank with a stereoscope. The shift of the shadow is almost imperceptible, but it was enough to make him suspect the structure was rotating.

(PRU) (see Appendix III) was anti-invasion missions. By then concern about German radar had reached the highest levels and Churchill became involved. He ordered an Enemy RDF Committee be set up under Air Marshal Joubert de la Ferte to get to the bottom of it.

Flying Officer W K Manifould.

The first PRU mission over Auderville returned with pictures of the field next to the enclosures. They showed an anti-aircraft gun and the pilot was not impressed having risked his life to get them. However, in the very edge of one picture was part of the structure Jones wanted photographing and he demanded another mission. On 22 February 1941, Flying Officer W K Manifould made a low oblique pass and returned with pictures of the *Freya* apparatus; the first obtained by the British of a German radar. The same day 120 MHz signals were picked up from Auderville and the

The picture taken by Flying Officer W K Manifould of the German *Freya* radar at Auderville 22 February 1941.

Danesfield House, which was RAF Medmenham from April 1941 until 1946. By 1945 it was dealing with an average of 25,000 negatives and 60,000 prints daily. It was only a few miles from RAF Benson from where the PRU aircraft operated.

location coincided with a bearing Garrard had taken in his car investigations.

On 24 February, Jones collected the Auderville pictures from Squadron Leader Claude Wavell of the Central Interpretation Unit (CIU) at Danesfield House, Medmenham in Buckinghamshire. Armed with them, and his other evidence, Jones attended the first meeting of Air Marshal Joubert de la Ferte's committee on the afternoon of 25 February. The evidence he presented was compelling; the Germans had radar, the enquiry was closed.

Knowing what they were looking for, both visually and electronically, made life much easier for the British. Within months, twenty-seven *Freyas* had been detected from Norway to southwest France and by the end of 1941, fifty *Freya* sites were known. Ultra intercepts mentioning equipment serial numbers led Jones to estimate there were about one hundred and fifty *Freyas* in existence. Signal traffic from the radar stations was intercepted and the codes were found to be very elementary and easily cracked. 109 Squadron Ferret Wellingtons flew towards the stations and by analysing the resultant signal traffic, it was relatively simple to work out at what range and height they were first detected. A picture was built up of the capability of the system and what its operators were seeing. Scientists devised counter-measures and very quickly the British were able to locate *Freya* and jam it or feed it false information.

The Vickers Wellington bomber entered service in 1938. Barnes Wallis, creator of the Dambusters' bouncing bomb, devised the Wellington's geodesic construction. Known as the Wimpy after the Popeye cartoon character, J Wellington Wimpy.

However, there was to be no time for complacency as Jones found evidence of a second system named *Würzburg*. Intelligence learned that a *Freya* was being sent to Rumania and two *Würzburg* radars to Bulgaria for coastal protection. The *Freya* would have to cover about 260 kms of Rumanian coastline. It was known *Freya* pulsed at 1,000 cycles per second and therefore the reflected pulse had to be received within a thousandth of a second to avoid interfering with the next pulse. Given the speed of radio waves, the range of *Freya* could be no more than 150 kms. The Bulgarian coast was 150 kms long; by deduction this meant each *Würzburg* had to have a range of at least 37.5 kms.

Jones believed *Freya* and *Würzburg* worked together. *Freya* had the range to give initial warning, but lacked precision. The range of *Würzburg* was shorter, but it was much more accurate and allowed controllers to vector night fighters onto targets. Jones' theory was correct. Unknown to the British at the time, a German First World War ace, General Ernst Udet, had experimented with two *Würzburg* radars, one plotting the target and the other his interceptor aircraft. In the summer of 1940 he made a successful interception of a practice target aircraft. The first British bomber intercepted by this method was on 16 October 1940. Bomber losses increased through 1941, particularly from night fighters. Jones wondered how was this happening, unless the fighters were directed by radar.

Ernst Udet – in the First World War he was second only to von Richthofen with 62 victories. Between the wars he was a stunt pilot and light aircraft manufacturer before becoming involved in developing the *Luftwaffe*. He became increasingly alcohol dependent and depressed, which resulted in him committing suicide in November 1941.

Freya, with its flat mattress-like antenna was unable to plot the altitude of an intruder and without altitude the air defence system would be ineffective at night. This added weight to Jones' theory that there was a second radar system. Intelligence learned of a 40 kms radius night-fighting area around Den Helder in the Netherlands, which suggested the range of this second radar was limited to 40 kms, very similar to the Bulgarian estimate of 37.5 kms. If so the pulse rate could not exceed 3,750 pulses per second.

In April 1941 transmissions of 570 MHz were picked up coming from France with a pulse rate of 3,750, i.e. consistent with a radar with a range of 40 kms. Ferret Wellingtons tracked these signals and on one tour along the coast of Brittany on 8 May, nine separate transmitters were detected. Nothing showed on subsequent photographic reconnaissance flights and it was concluded that the new radar had to be smaller than *Freya*, which had been hard enough to find. In September 1941 another night-fighter circle was identified near Bad Kreuznach in Germany, but this one was 60 kms in diameter. Had the *Würzburg* range been extended or was this yet another radar system?

In May 1941, a well wishing American at the embassy in Berlin sent the British a grainy picture of the top of a flak tower; it showed a metal lattice saucer on its edge. The picture took some months to reach Britain and its significance was not immediately apparent; perhaps it was just a searchlight. A Chinese scientist, who had worked in Berlin, was on his way home to China when he met the British Naval Attaché in Ankara. He was persuaded to divert to Britain in case he had useful information, but was not well treated by MI5 on arrival, as they did not appreciate the effort he had made to get there. He told Jones the American picture was taken in the Berlin Tiergarten. He described a parabolic mesh dish, which ruled out a searchlight, but Jones thought it might be a directional ranging device for flak guns.

The obscure picture taken by a member of the American embassy staff in Berlin in May 1941.

The roof of the Tiergarten flak tower is in the foreground. Behind, some 400 meres away is the command tower with the *Würzburg Riese* (Giant Würzburg) on the roof.

Jones obtained vertical reconnaissance pictures of the site from Claude Wavell and worked out the size of the dish. It was six metres across, which puzzled him, because he had not yet heard of the relatively new *Würzburg Riese* (Giant Würzburg), produced in response to Major General Josef Kammhuber's improvements to air defence (see Appendix III).

Jones was also puzzled because if *Würzburg* dishes were that size, why were reconnaissance flights not finding them? He thought the Germans might locate *Würzburg* with *Freya*, so he requested aerial reconnaissance missions concentrate on known *Freya* sites and went to RAF Benson to brief the PRU pilots on what to look for.

A close up of *Würzburg Riese*

On 15 November 1941, a PRU Spitfire on Sortie T/953 took

The Freya at Bruneval earlier in 1941. Such imagery is testament to the skill and courage of the PRU pilots. It was taken sideways while flying at 600 kph just below cliff top level with the sea barely 90 metres below.

The crucial photograph taken on Sortie T/953 on 15 November 1941. The new tracks and 'small black object' spotted by Charles Frank can just be made out.

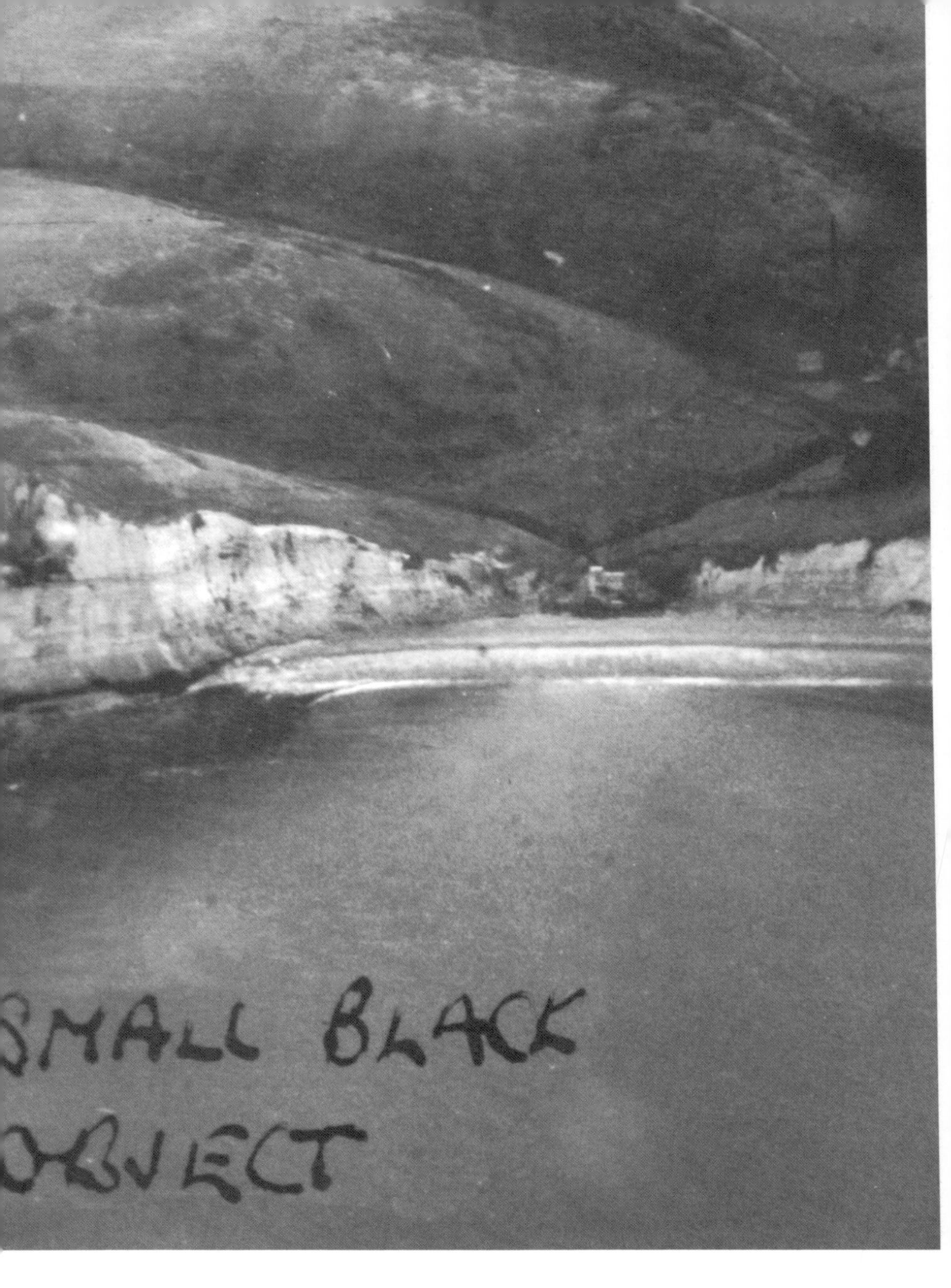
SMALL BLACK
OBJECT

photographs of a known *Freya* site on the cliff top at Cap d'Antifer close to Bruneval. The station had first been sighted in May 1941. Dr Charles Frank, on Jones' staff, noticed a new track had been trodden along the cliff edge from the *Freya* towards a large house (Manoir de la Falaise). Just before it reached the house it swung right ending at a 'small black object' halfway between the house and cliff edge. Could the object be part of the *Freya*, or was it the elusive *Würzburg*? Jones asked for clearer pictures through official channels, but also tipped off Claude Wavell unofficially what he needed.

Flight Lieutenant Tony Hill – the pilot who obtained the close up images of the Bruneval *Würzburg*. He was shot down on 18 October 1942 on a low level operation over Le Creusot and his back was broken. The Resistance rescued him, but he died on 21 October while being carried to a rescue aircraft sent to recover him. Hill is buried in Dijon les Pejoces Communal Cemetery. R V Jones was very saddened by his death.

On 3 December, two PRU pilots, Flight Lieutenants Tony Hill and Gordon Hughes, visited the CIU at Danesfield, fifteen miles from Benson, to discuss low-level photography of radar sites. Claude Wavell showed them the pictures from the 15 November Bruneval mission and pointed out the small black object. Hill had been involved in numerous missions over possible radar stations and, having looked at the pictures and hearing about the problem with bomber losses, told Wavell he would go to Bruneval and get the answer.

Hill took off the next day, flew low over Bruneval and got out again. On returning he discovered that his camera had failed when photographing the small black object, although he did bring back valuable pictures of changes at the *Freya* site. However, Hill was able to confirm by telephone to Wavell that the object was like, 'an electric bowl fire about ten feet (three metres) across'. If correct, he had probably found the origin of the 570 MHz transmissions. Despite the risks, Hill said he would return the next day, 5 December. Jones' official request had at last made its way through the system and other pilots at Benson were preparing for the mission. Hill made it very clear that this one was his and if he saw them within twenty miles of Bruneval he would shoot them down. However, he wasn't clear on how he would achieve this, as that day

The remarkable front and side views (overleaf) of the Bruneval *Würzburg* taken by Tony Hill 5 December 1941.

he flew Spitfire PR.IV R7044, which was unarmed.

This time he returned with photographs of the site that confirmed everything he said the day before. The very clear front and side pictures of the *Würzburg* allowed the size of the dish to be assessed. Although this did not prove beyond doubt that the radar transmitted on 570 MHz, at three metres across the dish was consistent with a radar operating at that frequency with a range of 40 kms. A system like it based upon a six metres dish would have a range of 60 kms provided the pulse rate was dropped from 3,750 to 2,500, i.e. the *Würzburg Reise*. Jones reported his findings to the Assistant Chief of Air Staff (Intelligence) (ACAS (I) on 12 December in a two-page memo. ACAS (I) immediately alerted the Secretary of State for Air, the Chief of Air Staff (CAS), Vice Chief of Air Staff (VCAS) and others; Jones' memo became the catalyst for the Bruneval Raid.

In order to effectively neutralize *Würzburg* by counter-

S.(I).

A new type of German R.D.F. station has been photograph
ote will outline the factors which led to its discovery.

A normal 120 Mc/sec. German R.D.F. station had been
since May, 1941, to exist in the neighbourhood of Cap
fer (15 km. north of Le Havre). Its appearance was
to resemble that at Audeville, which had been photographed
2.41, as a result of successful cooperation between No.1
, C.I.U. (then P.I.U.), and my own branch (then S.R.3.).
ultimately discovered a station at Cap d'Antifer, which A
led expectations, on photograph No.021 of sortie T/953 of
41 (attached). This showed two of the usual emplacements
further search revealed the fact that the station had been
ntally covered on an earlier sortie, T/353 of 2.8.41. B

During our study of the layout of the station, it was
d out by Dr. Frank that a path led from the main
ements towards the building (believed to have been a hotel)
he centre of the photograph 023 of T/953 (attached) C but
he path terminated in a loop just short of the building.
end of this loop was a small black object, which must
ore be an object of interest to the personnel of the main
n. By this time we knew that sortie T/353 gave better
and so the appropriate photograph (No.08 attached) was
for, and at the same time C.I.U. was informed of our
ions which agreed with their own. The last photograph,
gh of larger scale, was still indistinct.

On 3.12.41, Flight Lieutenant Hill, D.F.C., a P.R.U.
happened to be visiting C.I.U., and incidentally
ssed the problem of dicing radio stations with Squadron
Wavell of that Unit. Flight Lieutenant Hill had some
ago diced the Knickebein transmitter at Bergen-op-Zoom, but
luck the target had only appeared on the edge of two
raphs. He thought, however, that he now knew the
ary technique for getting the target in the centre.
on Leader Wavell pointed out to him that we were very
sted in the suspicious object at Cap d'Antifer, which we
t might be a new type of R.D.F. equipment, resembling an
ric bowl fire.

Flight Lieutenant Hill went out the next day, on sortie
to photograph the station. He returned apologetically,
only succeeded in photographing one of the main
cements, (photograph No.04 attached). This photograph
een of considerable value, because it shows that the older
of station has been modified by lifting the lower frame
contact with the top, possibly when the stations are
ed from 1000 to 500 cycles repetition rate for increased
. The aerial now has a square appearance, instead of two

separate rectangles, which explains why we have recently had several reports of square aerials, which we had thought might belong to the newer 53 cm. stations. Flight Lieutenant Hill had, in addition, been able to see the unidentified object, and reported that it did in fact look like a large electric fire.

On the following morning, he went out again; his results (photographs No.03 and 04 of sortie A/30, enlargements attached) F G are certainly the finest that have yet been obtained for us, although we have had some extremely good ones in the past. It is a remarkable achievement to have obtained two views at right angles well placed on two successive photographs, with so little trace of movement.

It is impossible yet to be absolutely definite, but the apparatus photographed is very probably one of the 53 cm. R.D.F. stations which have been heard for some months: the photographing of such a station was the most important object of our immediate programme. This particular model is used for aircraft reporting, although another modification exists for G.L. The paraboloid and cabin, which are mounted on a trolley in a shallow pit, have rotated between the two photographs, and the vertical dipole in front of the paraboloid can be clearly seen. The apparatus can determine heights by tilting the paraboloid to point the beam at the target aircraft, and so measuring the range and elevation. It may be used in conjunction with the main station which can only determine range.

These excellent photographs are a very valuable contribution to our study of the enemy's night defences, for they have provided us with positive knowledge which can be obtained in no other way. In addition to their striking testimony to the skill of the pilot, and to the staff of P.R.U., they represent the culmination of a long chase in which the cooperation of A.D.Ph.I., P.R.U., and C.I.U., has been generously and enthusiastically extended to my own branch.

R.V. Jones.

12.12.41. A.D.I.(Science)

ADI (Sc)
I have shown this to S. of S. CAS. VCAS & DCAS.
All express admiration for the results
obtained from all concerned.
[illegible]
14/12.

R V Jones' 12 December 1941 memo to ACAS (I) – the catalyst for the Bruneval Raid.

Commodore, later Admiral of the Fleet Louis Francis Albert Victor Nicholas George Mountbatten, 1st Earl Mountbatten of Burma.

In October 1941 he replaced Admiral Roger Keyes as Chief of Combined Operations. He was later Supreme Allied Commander South East Asia, the last Viceroy of India and its first Governor-General following independence. First Sea Lord 1954-59 was followed by six years as Chief of the Defence Staff, during which he consolidated the single service departments into a unified Ministry of Defence. He was murdered by the IRA in 1979.

measures, Jones and his team needed to study one of the systems, or at least its vital pieces of technology. Below the Bruneval installation and about 400 metres away was a beach; the idea of dispatching a raid to retrieve the *Würzburg* from its exposed position was born.

Jones talked to W B Lewis, Deputy Superintendent of TRE Worth, who supported the idea. It was picked up by VCAS, Sir Richard Peirse, and Lindemann, which meant the idea soon reached Churchill. It quickly passed from Air Intelligence through the Air Staff to HQ Combined Operations.

Chief Combined Ops (CCO), Lord Louis Mountbatten, had formed a new Intelligence Section at Christmas 1941 tasked specifically with looking for suitable targets in France. On 1 January 1942 the Section alerted him to Bruneval. Mountbatten and his staff studied the problem and concluded that the extensive coastal defences precluded a landing from seaward by commandos. Such an approach would be costly in casualties and too slow to capture the *Würzburg* before it could be destroyed. As surprise and speed were the essential requirements, an airborne assault was the only viable method of insertion. After completing the operation the raiders could be taken off by landing craft, having overcome the beach defences from the rear.

On 8 January, Mountbatten contacted Major General Boy Browning, commanding the Airborne Division, and Group Captain Sir Nigel Norman, commander of the newly formed troop carrying 38 Wing RAF. He asked them if they could cooperate in conducting such a raid; both agreed. Browning was particularly enthusiastic as a successful operation would be a boost to the airborne troops and a demonstration of their value.

The two commanders believed the training of troops and

aircrews could be completed by the end of February, which coincided with the conditions necessary for the operation. These were a full moon for visibility and a rising tide to allow the landing craft to manoeuvre in shallow water. Possible dates were between the nights of 22nd/23rd and 25/26 February or a delay of a month would be incurred. On 14 January, 1st Parachute Brigade received warning that a company of infantry and a sapper section would be required with reinforcements.

Major General, later Lieutenant General Sir Frederick (Boy) Browning – fought on the Western Front with the Grenadier Guards from 1915 and served alongside Major Winston Churchill for a period. He was the first Sandhurst Adjutant to ride his horse up the steps of Old College at the end of the Sovereign's Parade in 1926. In 1928 he was an Olympic bobsleigher and married the author Daphne du Maurier in 1932.

Security was paramount and a cover story was invented to account for the training and preparations. Despite this, staff officers not in the know asked awkward questions why scarce equipments were being demanded, until they were told there was an urgent operational requirement. The clearance of beaches on the south coast for training also raised eyebrows. GHQ Home Forces almost blew the cover by mentioning in a letter on 28 January that British paratroopers were about to take part in an operation. Despite this and a number of other breaches of security, the enemy was not alerted.

Planning conferences were held at HQ Combined Operations on 12th, 19th and 29 January. Mountbatten took the proposal to the Chiefs of Staff Committee on 21 January and they approved the raid, codenamed Operation BITING.

The once Combined Operations HQ at Richmond Terrace in Westminster from the Embankment. The white building to the right is the Foreign Office on Whitehall.

Sir Henry Nigel Norman seated front left while serving with 601 (County of London) Squadron Auxiliary Air Force in 1932. Roger Bushell, mastermind of the Great Escape in March 1944, is top right. Norman served with the Royal Garrison Artillery until March 1918 when he was seconded to the Royal Engineers Signals Service and later Royal Signals. In 1928 he co-founded Airwork Services and the company opened Heston Aerodrome. In 1935 he co-founded Norman and Dawbarn, responsible for laying out Gatwick, Birmingham, Ringway, Jersey and Guernsey airports. Early in the war he commanded 110 Wing and the Central Landing Establishment at Ringway and was the Air Force commander on the first British parachute raid at Tragino, Italy in 1941.

Chapter Three

INTELLIGENCE

IN PARIS on 24 January 1942, Free French resistance agent Robert Delattre (codename Bob) received two radio messages from London. They were decoded that evening by Gilbert Renault (Remy) and his wife Edith at a rented flat on Avenue de la Motte-Picquet. London needed information on Bruneval, but in getting it, Remy was not to endanger himself, the network or the scheduled pick-up to take him to London in the next full moon period. In the event that an agent was taken, he must be given a number of other locations on the coast so the Germans would be unsure what it was all about. The specific information required was the position and number of machine guns, the location of barbed wire and other defences and the type of troops in the area and their preparedness.

One of Remy's agents was Roger Dumont (Pol), an air force officer who ran the *Luftwaffe* section. He was appointed to lead the reconnaissance, which was estimated would take two weeks. One of Pol's friends, Roger Herisse, another air force officer, was the first to spot the *Freya* radar station at Bruneval. Pol and Remy studied the maps and concluded they should not try to get near the installation.

Gilbert Renault (Remy)

When France fell he refused to accept the armistice and went to London with his youngest brother on board a trawler. Remy went back to France via Portugal and Spain to create a network centred on the Atlantic coast. He was a monarchist and a deeply religious man and, believing his resistance organisation was favoured by God, named it Confrérie Notre-Dame (CND). When the Réseau Saint-Jacques network was infiltrated and destroyed, Remy took it over as well, including the French north coast from Brest to Dunkirk. CND eventually had 1,375 members.

Charles Chauveau's garage on the D940 Le Havre to Étratat road.

Roger Dumont (Pol).

Roger Herisse on the left meeting General Charles de Gaulle.

At the end of January, Charles Chauveau (Charlemagne), a garage owner from Le Havre, went to Paris to pick up Pol. They took rooms in a seedy, unheated hotel in Le Havre that was so damp, Pol tried to sleep on a chair rather than in the bed. Charlemagne borrowed two tyres with chains as he heard the roads around Bruneval were covered in thick snow and ice.

They drove north out of Le Havre on the N40 (now the D940), then through Heuqueville and Saint-Jouin to the Calvary road junction at the eastern end of Bruneval. The first building on the left was the Hotel Beauminet owned by Paul Vennier and his Swiss wife. They knew Vennier was sympathetic and would have some information, so they parked behind the hotel and went in. Vennier confirmed there were *Luftwaffe* personnel living at the farm complex known as Le Presbytère (Theuville on modern maps), but he did not know what was at the chateau (Manoir de la Falaise close to the *Wurzburg*); no one was allowed near it. A platoon under an efficient sergeant lived in the Hotel. It manned a guard post in

Hotel Beauminet.

The Calvary road junction at the eastern edge of Bruneval.Le Havre is to the left, the beach straight on and the road behind leads to La Poterie.

The cellars of the demolished chateau with the wooded farm complex of Le Presbytère in the background.

the house named Stella Maris on the beach, with two bunkers nearby each containing machine guns. These defences were not manned permanently, but could be quickly by the ten soldiers who lived close by at all times. The troops were of good quality and alert.

Pol suggested to Charlemagne they look at the beach and Vennier told them it was out of bounds and mined. They walked down the hill to the barbed wire entanglement across the road. On the left a German guard emerged from the doorway of Stella Maris. Charlemagne buttered him up, saying his cousin was normally shut up in an office in Paris and would love to see the sea before he went home. The sentry smiled and Charlemagne continued, saying they were lucky he was there as they had heard there were mines; the sentry confirmed there were. When Charlemagne asked if he would mind escorting them to the beach, he was pleased to oblige. He pulled aside the knife rest to let them through, replaced it and had them follow him closely on the path through the minefield.

On the steeply shelving pebble beach they noted the swell, but as it was low tide they could see there were no underwater obstacles. Charlemagne gave the German a cigarette while Pol appeared to be dreaming, but in reality he was taking in the scene. South of Stella Maris and just above its roof level was a

Stella Maris stood on the site of the modern building on the left. This is where Pol and Charlemagne persuaded the German sentry to let them onto the beach just beyond the concrete wall (post-raid) at the end of the road.

machine-gun emplacement. To the north and higher up was another, in which he could see the sentry. There was no barbed wire after the road barricade. On the way back the German took no precautions walking through the minefield, so they knew it was fake.

Back at the hotel they chatted with the clients. Many were Charlemagne's customers so it provided an excellent cover for their visit. After a glass of Calvados they drove inland to Hotel des Vieux Plats in Gonneville-la-Mallet and had a celebratory black market lunch, washed down with real coffee and more Calvados. Pol then copied the German names in the visitors' book, so London would be able to trace their units.

On 9th February, Remy met Pol at the house of Madame Lucienne Dixon, a French woman married to an American, at 1 Rue General Largeau near the Porte d'Auteuil in Paris. Pol and Remy condensed the details of the reconnaissance into a

Hotel des Vieux Plats in Gonneville-la-Mallet pre-war:

short message to avoid the very efficient detector vans. Remy took the message home where he checked and rechecked the coding before his operator (Bob) took it away to be transmitted later that evening to London. This information, added to the PRU air photographs and topographical details, produced the following detailed intelligence assessment:

The Würzburg, *mounted in a pit about fifty metres from the cliff, was surrounded by barbed wire and a number of dugouts, including a machine gun post on the cliff edge.*

There was an isolated chateau fifty metres inland from the Würzburg *with possibly twenty signalers and guards living there.*

To the north a wooded farm enclosure (Le Presbytère), housed approximately 100 troops, including those who manned the Freya.

Between the Freya *and* Würzburg *were two weapon pits.*

Three new blockhouses connected by communications trenches were being built on the northern cliff 200 metres from the radar.

South of the beach road was a strong point with a pillbox at its centre covering the beach and inland; it was believed to contain four machine guns and was organised for all round defence.

The Bruneval platoon of about thirty soldiers manned the defences guarding the beach and lived in the Hotel du Beauminet 500 metres inland.

The house closest to the beach, Stella Maris, contained two machine guns and was surrounded by wire ten metres thick; ten soldiers from the Bruneval platoon manned it permanently.

Stella Maris and beach pre-war.

The beach was not mined, but the entrance was thickly wired and it was patrolled regularly.

There appeared to be a pillbox protected by wire just off the shore.

There was a machine gun post and more wire 100 metres along the road towards Bruneval.

A mobile reserve of infantry was believed to be close by at La Poterie.

Further reserves were believed to be at one hour's notice at Étretat, about eight kms away.

A reconnaissance battalion with armoured cars was twenty-five kilometres to the east at Yebleron; the first could arrive within one hour.

The various positions were given codenames for ease of identification by the raiders:

REDOUBT – three new bunkers on the northern cliff.
BEACH FORT – roadblock and the two bunkers above and on the beach.
GUARD ROOM – the house Stella Maris.
LONE HOUSE – the chateau on the cliffs.
HENRY – *Würzburg*.
RECTANGLE – Le Presbytère farm enclosure.

The main features of the Bruneval battlefield.

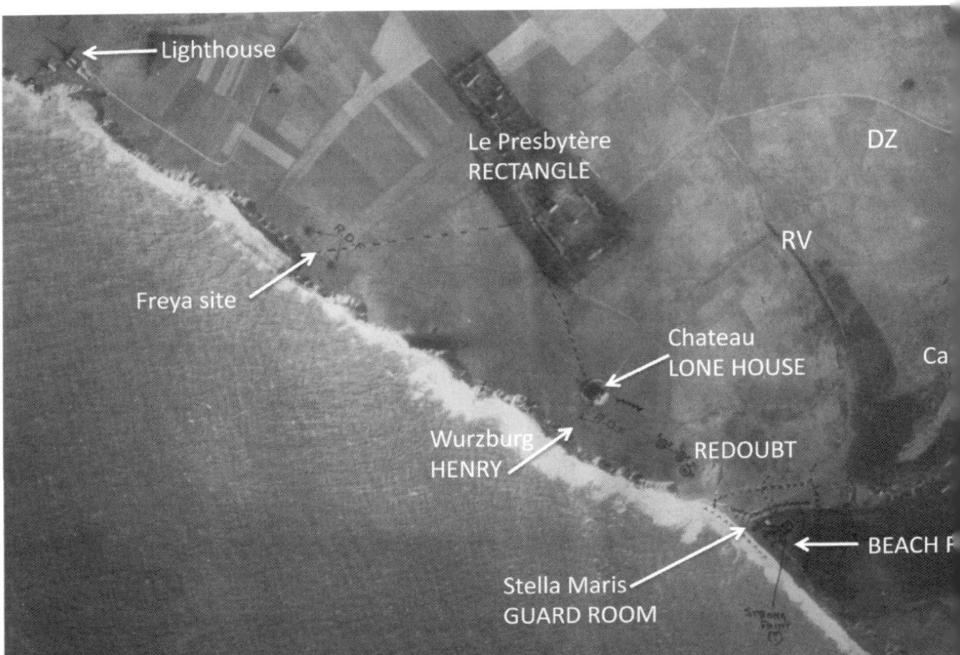

The Armstrong Whitworth Whitley bomber entered service in March 1937. It cruised at 185 mph and with a full bomb load was limited to 470 miles. The last Whitley bombing raid was on Ostend on 29/30 April 1942, following which they were used by Coastal Command and as paratrooper trainers and glider tugs.

twelve aircraft available, the parachute force was limited to 120 men. Within this ceiling there was to be a section of Royal Engineers, a radar engineer, an interpreter and four signalers.

The mission was defined in priority order to:

1. Capture parts of HENRY and return with them.
2. Capture prisoners (officers and technical personnel) who operated HENRY.
3. Obtain other information about HENRY and documents relating to it.

The aircraft would approach from the south and drop the parachute force onto a Drop Zone (DZ) about 800 metres inland. On the ground, the raiders would rendezvous (RV) on a track by a line of trees in a re-entrant, 600 metres from LONE HOUSE. Once assembled the three groups, all named after famous Admirals, would disperse to their respective tasks.

NELSON's four sections (forty men) were to seize and hold the beach. They had the farthest to travel and accordingly were first to drop at 0015. In order to maintain surprise they were not to make any noise until the attack on LONE HOUSE and HENRY began. One section would move directly to the northern cliff to seize REDOUBT, another would move south against the pillbox and trenches at GUARD ROOM, while the third worked its way towards BEACH FORT down the centre of the ravine. A

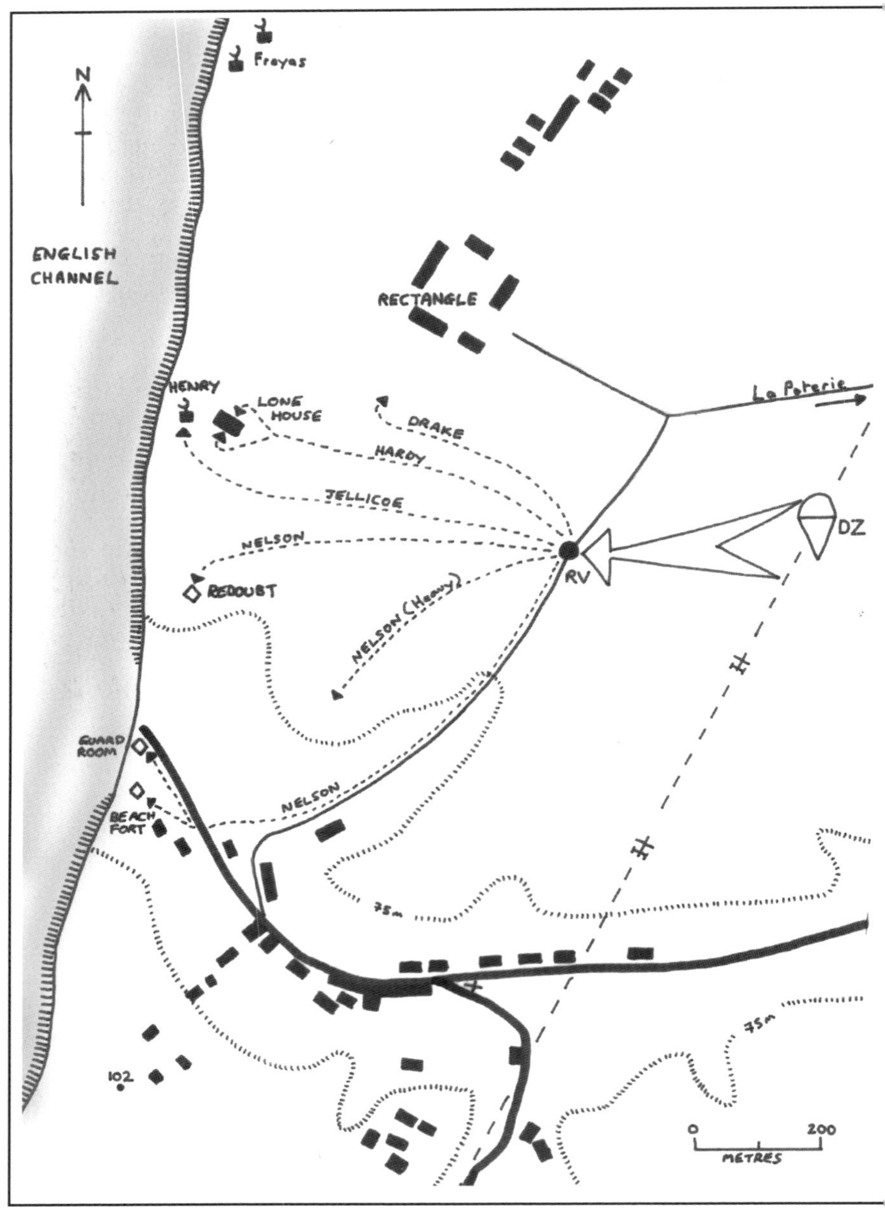

The plan for the assault on the radar station and the beach. Wooded areas have been omitted for clarity, but much of the terrain from 75 metres downwards was and still is covered in trees. RODNEY is not shown, its positions were about 200 metres west of the RV.

Looking north up the cliffs towards REDOUBT on the skyline. A later concrete pillbox is just visible at the highest point with a narrow track leading towards it. In the foreground the memorial covers the remains of GUARD ROOM.

Looking from REDOUBT down towards the beach. BEACH FORT is the building closest to the beach at the end of the ravine. Above it is the memorial on the site of GUARD ROOM. Both were to be assaulted from the left.

The spur to be occupied by NELSON's heavy section looking from GUARD ROOM.

fourth, heavy section, under the Company Second-in-Command (2IC) was to take up position on the spur east of REDOUBT, from where it would cover the road and provide fire support to the other sections. When the positions had been taken, two sappers in the heavy section were to lay anti-tank mines on the road 200 metres inland to slow any attempt by the Germans to rush the beach in vehicles. They were then to move to the beach and tape a path through the minefield, if one was found. The 2IC was to set up a checkpoint on the beach to control the evacuation and would be joined by signalers to contact the Navy. The NELSON sections to north and south, i.e. those at REDOUBT and GUARD ROOM were to remain in position while the rest of the force fell back to the beach.

HARDY (forty men) was subdivided into JELLICOE, HARDY and DRAKE. These sections were to drop at 0020 and from the RV would move directly to LONE HOUSE and HENRY. DRAKE (ten men) would take up a blocking position between LONE HOUSE and RECTANGLE, but remain silent until required or ordered to make a diversion during the withdrawal. The signal to commence the attack would be four whistle blasts, at which:

JELLICOE (ten men) – would secure HENRY, following which two sappers were to collect wiring diagrams and documents and, if no-one else arrived, dismantle the set as best they could.

HARDY (twenty men) – fourteen men with the company commander would secure LONE HOUSE and collect prisoners on the ground floor. Then a four-man dismantling party, divided into two pairs in case of casualties, would go forward to HENRY to identify the components and dismantle the radar. The final man in HARDY was the interpreter. As it would be impossible to remove all the radar parts, instructions were given on which elements would be most useful. First the dismantling party was to sketch the layout and take pictures before removal began. The antenna from the centre of the dish would prove whether this set was responsible for the 570 MHz transmissions. They were then to work backwards starting at the receiver and display equipment, which would reveal if the set included anti-jamming devices. The transmitter would show how well the set performed. It would help if prisoners could be taken, especially a radar operator. If any equipment was impossible to remove the sappers were to rip off the identification labels. They would have less than thirty minutes to carry out their tasks.

RODNEY (forty men) would drop at 0025. It was to be positioned to cover likely enemy approaches in order to block counter-attacks and act as the rearguard when the force withdrew to the beach. Two sections were to position themselves where they could bring fire to bear upon the southern side of RECTANGLE and stop any interference from it. The other two sections were to be ready to stop attacks from the village and were to position themselves west of the RV. The commander was to ensure the sappers and signalers in the group got to the beach to meet up with the 2IC.

A sixth group, NOAH was on the evacuation landing craft. If conditions allowed and the parachute force commander gave permission, a TRE radar expert would dash to the *Würzburg* to make a technical assessment. In case the raid failed, his landing craft was equipped with a receiver to confirm if the 570 MHz transmissions were coming from Bruneval.

When HARDY withdrew to the beach with the radar

components it would be followed at fifty metres intervals by JELLICOE and DRAKE. RODNEY was to be the rearguard and would be called in by radio (each group had a 38 Set, working on 8 MHz), or runner when the other groups had arrived at the beach. Commanders of each section were to report anyone missing to the 2IC on arrival. Four battalion signalers would establish a report centre and set up a homing beacon and 18 Set on 8.7 MHz to contact the Navy. These signalers would travel one in each RODNEY aircraft and the two radios and two beacons were also split up in case of loss or damage in the drop. As soon as naval forces were heard approaching the beach, transmissions were to cease and a white torch was to guide them in. If the 18 Sets did not work or failed to arrive, then one of the 38 Sets would be used instead. Very (flare) pistols were to indicate the beach by firing flares right and left along the base of the cliffs.

The new and unfamiliar 38 Set radio. There were mixed reports about its efficiency after the raid.

The larger and more powerful 18 Set mounted on a backpack.

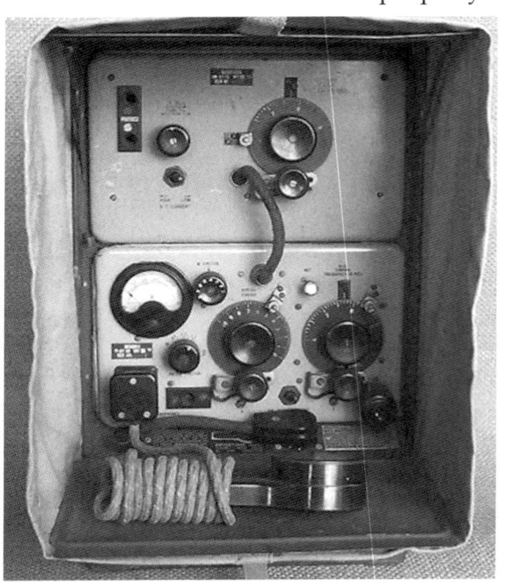

The 2IC was to ensure the boats were properly loaded in the correct order and inform the naval commander when they were ready to leave. It was emphasised rather chillingly, that only signaler prisoners would be brought back. Sentries would be dealt with silently if possible and ammunition was to be conserved. NELSON would be the last to be evacuated.

The password was to be, rather unsurprisingly, Biting! All ranks were impressed with the importance of recovering HENRY; without it the raid would be a failure.

Chapter Five

ASSEMBLING THE FORCE

WITH THE MAIN PARTS of the plan in place, the assembly of the force commenced. There were separate maritime, land and air elements, each with its own component commander:

Naval forces – Commander Frederick N Cook Royal Australian Navy (RAN).

Parachute landing force – Major John D Frost.

Air forces – Group Captain Sir Nigel Norman.

Major John Dutton Frost – born in India, son of General F D Frost. He was commissioned into the Cameronians in September 1932 and spent the early years of the war with the Iraq Levies. He returned to Sussex on coastal defence duties before joining 2nd Parachute Battalion.

rederick Cook joined the AN aged 13 and served or 42 years. He survived ne sinking of HMS *Royal Oak* by U-*47* in Scapa low in October 1939 and ne sinking of HMS *Curlew* off Norway in May 940. In July 1940 he set p HMS *Tormentor*, a ombined Operations aval training base at the lousehold Brigade Yacht lub at Warsash on the lamble.

Commander Cook was summoned to a meeting at Combined Operations HQ in London in mid-January. The senior Royal Navy officer, Captain John Hughes-Hallett DSO, briefed him that he would lead the naval force on a forthcoming raid. The main difficulty facing the naval forces was finding the tiny beach at Bruneval after 160 kms of dead reckoning, as there were no navigation points after the Isle of Wight. Cook borrowed Taut-wire measuring gear from the Hydro-graphers and had it fitted to the stern of the landing craft mother ship. This apparatus consisted of a weight attached to piano wire dropped over the stern. The wire paid out as the journey progressed

Captain (later Vice-Admiral) John Hughes-Hallett played an important role in planning cross-Channel raids and was the Naval Commander at Dieppe in August 1942. He may have been the proposer of the Mulberry Harbour and was Naval COS to the Overlord planners. He commanded Assault Force J during the Normandy landings. A strict disciplinarian, he was known as 'Hughes-Hitler'.

HMS *Prins Albert*, a Belgian ferry on the Ostend-Dover route built in 1937. When Germany invaded she was taken over by the Ministry of War Transport. In 1941 she was rebuilt as an armed auxiliary transport carrying 8 x ALCs and took part in operations at the Lofoten Islands, Dieppe, Sicily, Italy, Normandy (OMAHA), Southern France and Rangoon. In addition to her crew she could carry 340 troops. Known as 'Lucky Albert', she was never hit and returned to service on the Ostend-Dover route until 1968.

Bren light machine gun – standard support weapon in the infantry rifle section. Based on a Czech design produced at Brno and manufactured by the Royal Small Arms Factory at Enfield, hence Bren. It fired the standard .303 rifle cartridge from a thirty-round box magazine or a 100-round pan magazine. It was extremely accurate out to 600 metres and fired 500 rounds per minute.

The 0.55-inch Boys Anti-Tank Rifle was able to penetrate light tanks early in the war, but was impotent against the heavier armour of later models. It was bolt action with a five-round box magazine. The rifle was large and heavy with considerable recoil. Although redundant as an anti-armour weapon, during the Korean War the US Marine Corps converted some to long-range sniper rifles.

enabling the distance travelled to be measured very accurately, but it was of no help in maintaining direction.

Cook's force for the operation consisted of:

HMS *Prins Albert*, commanded by Lieutenant Commander H B Peate RNR, carrying six ALCs and two similar Landing Craft Support (LSC).

Five MGBs from the 14th Flotilla commanded by Lieutenant Commander W G Everitt RN.

Thirty-two soldiers from No.12 Commando to provide covering fire from the landing craft during the evacuation – four men per landing craft each armed with a Bren or a Boys anti-tank rifle.

An officer and 20 Royal Army Medical Corps (RAMC) soldiers to treat casualties on the return.

Four Free French and two British escort destroyers.

Donald Preist, the TRE radar expert.

Most elements of the naval force were already in the Solent area. The exception was HMS *Prins Albert*, which was moored off Inveraray in Scotland. One of its landing craft would carry the TRE radar expert, Donald Preist, who held a commission as a Flight Lieutenant in the Royal Air Force Volunteer Reserve (RAFVR), and the Airborne Division Liaison Officer, Major Peter Bromley-Martin Grenadier Guards. If conditions allowed they would dash to the *Würzburg* to make a technical assessment.

Hardwick Hall, a magnificent Elizabethan country house, built for Bess of Hardwick, set on a hilltop near Chesterfield in Derbyshire. In late 1941, 2nd and 3rd Parachute Battalions formed there. When 1st Parachute Brigade left Hardwick for Bulford on Salisbury Plain later in 1942, it became the Airborne Forces Depot.

If for any reason Cook felt he needed to abort the operation, he had to make this decision before 2200 on the night of the raid, the take off time for the jump aircraft. Thereafter it would be almost impossible to recall them before they dropped the paratroopers.

On 14 January, Major General Boy Browning and the commander of 1st Parachute Brigade, Brigadier Richard Gale, were tasked to provide an infantry company plus a section of sappers. At this time The Airborne Division (later 1st Airborne Division) was composed of only two parachute battalions in 1st Parachute Brigade. Only the 1st Parachute Battalion was fully trained and Browning wished to keep it intact in case a larger operation came along, so the 2nd Parachute Battalion, forming at Hardwick Hall near Chesterfield, was ordered to provide the company plus reinforcements. A Royal Engineer (RE) officer and eleven sappers were also tasked, including a small reserve.

The parachute landing force would come directly under command of HQ Airborne Division during the training period and Major Bromley-Martin was appointed liaison officer between the HQ and the parachute landing force. Bromley-Martin was a legend in the Division due to his account of his first parachute jump during which he jumped fourth behind Major H O Wright:

The next recollection I have is of Major Wright with parachute open and canopy fully filled, some 150 feet above me. My parachute, sir, had not then fully opened, and I had the gravest doubts as to whether it would function before it had been repacked. I was unable to devise a method of repacking it in the limited time at my disposal. As I was also unable to think of any satisfactory means of assisting the contraption to perform the functions which I had been led to suppose were automatic; in my submission I had no alternative but to fall earthwards at, I believe, the rate of 32 fps, accelerating to the maximum speed of 176 fps... This I did.... and having dropped a certain distance, my parachute suddenly opened, and I made a very light landing.

Lieutenant Colonel Edwin William Conquest Flavell was one of only a few airborne soldiers who fought in both World Wars. In the First he commanded 126th Machine Gun Company in Flanders, being awarded the MC and Bar, and served with Lieutenant Richard Gale, who commanded 6th Airborne Division in the Second. In April 1942, Flavell left 2nd Parachute Battalion to take command of 1st Parachute Brigade, which he led in North Africa and was awarded the DSO. He later commanded 6th Airlanding Brigade in Normandy.

Captain John Frost joined 2nd Parachute Battalion as the Adjutant at Hardwick on 29 September 1941. Towards the end of the year he and the Commanding Officer (CO), Lieutenant Colonel Edward Flavell MC, completed two balloon jumps, but Frost spent time in hospital afterwards with a knee injury sustained on landing. After New Year leave he returned to Hardwick to learn he was to take over C Company from Major Philip Teichman, one of the few Englishmen in what was known as 'Jock Company'. Teichman was to move to B

Sticks of trainee paratroopers forming up at RAF Ringway.

Company. The moves were caused by officers being posted out to form other battalions and because one of the company commanders wasn't up to the job.

Both B and C Companies had completed their parachute training when the order came to send a company to Tilshead on Salisbury Plain for a demonstration of airborne capability. C Company was the best trained in the Battalion. The CO told Frost, if he completed his jumps course inside a week, he would lead C Company. In case Frost could not be trained in time, around 16 January Teichman went ahead to Tilshead with the Company Quartermaster Sergeant (CQMS) as the advance party. Both Frost and Teichman very much wanted the command.

Frost went to Ringway and realised from the preferential treatment he received that there might be more to the demonstration than met the eye. Bad weather delayed his jumps and he completed the course with only hours to spare. He dashed back to Hardwick, took command of C Company on 24 January and headed with it to Tilshead by train. He was met by a disgruntled Teichman; Frost sympathised, but not too much.

As part of the security cover, the Battalion war diary records that C Company left Hardwick 25 January for Ringway to take part in a scheme. Tilshead (or Westdown) Camp was where the Glider Pilot Regiment was forming, so the arrival of a parachute

Tilshead (Westdown) Camp, on Salisbury Plain. The Hostilities Only accommodation is still being used as a training camp some sixty-six years later.

company did not raise undue interest. C Company should have arrived there on the 21st, but heavy snow delayed the move. The day after arrival Browning came to inspect. Frost dreaded this, as the men were very scruffy after a period of intensive training and Browning, a Grenadier, was a stickler for discipline. Browning told Frost to ask for anything he needed through the liaison officer... including a new uniform for every man as they were the dirtiest company he'd ever seen.

Frost was restricted to 120 men for the landing force, the capacity of the twelve jump aircraft. Nine of these places would be filled by sappers from 1st Parachute Field Squadron RE. Four more places were filled by battalion signallers and there was also a RAF Flight Sergeant and an interpreter. There were therefore only 105 places for infantry troops. When C Company left Hardwick it was accompanied by part of B Company. On 8 February, the strength of the Tilshead detachment from 2nd Parachute Battalion was 157 (eight officers and 149 other ranks). This means around forty-eight men from 2nd Parachute Battalion who went through the training did not take part in the raid.

Netheravon airfield – in use since 1912, is probably the longest continuously operated airfield in the world. In January 1942, 38 Wing RAF formed there, to support airborne forces; it expanded to nine squadrons and became 38 Group before D-Day.

Wing Commander Percy Charles Pickard – he farmed in Kenya and while driving back to England with three friends nearly died of malaria. Commissioned in January 1937 he fought over Norway, France and during the Dunkirk evacuation. In the 1941 Crown Film Unit, 'Target for Tonight' he was Squadron Leader Dickson, pilot of Wellington 'F for Freddie'.

38 Wing RAF in Army Cooperation Command was formed on 15 January 1942 to support airborne operations. The Wing was commanded by Group Captain Sir Nigel Norman. At that time it consisted of 296 and 297 Squadrons based at Netheravon on Salisbury Plain, but neither was ready for immediate operations. As a result on 25 January, 51 Squadron in Bomber Command under Wing Commander Charles Pickard was selected for the raid, with Norman in overall command.

A year before, on 10-11 February 1941, British paratroopers from 11th Special Air Service Battalion (formed from No.2 Commando), had dropped into southern Italy to destroy the Tragino aqueduct; Operation COLOSSUS was the first British airborne operation. They jumped from Whitleys of 78 Squadron, but 51 Squadron crews flew some of the aircraft. It is possible that 51 Squadron was chosen for Operation BITING because of this previous experience. Based at Dishforth in Yorkshire, it began training under the guidance of Squadron Leader Warne DFC of 38 Wing. Around 6 February, the Squadron was brought south for the operation to Thruxton, just off the A303 in Hampshire. The crews were accommodated at nearby RAF Andover.

Thruxton airfield from the west. Part of it is now a racetrack.

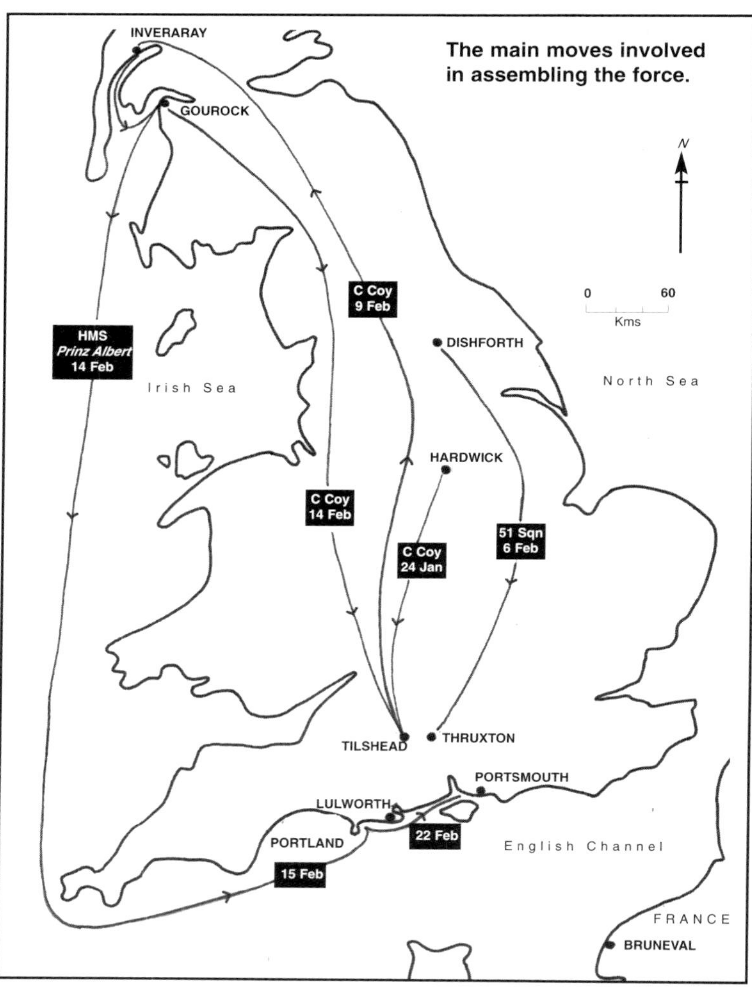

In addition to the jump aircraft, a number of other air assets were involved in the operation:

Bomber Command launched a number of diversionary operations prior to the raid.

Special reconnaissance missions were flown just before the raid to check the sea state and visibility.

Fighter Command flew a diversionary mission on the night of the raid.

Spitfire cover was provided during daylight on the return sea journey by 11 Group of Fighter Command.

Chapter Six

TRAINING & PREPARATIONS

THE MORNING after Browning's visit to Tilshead, Frost and his officers were briefed by Bromley-Martin that they were to take part in a demonstration of an airborne raid for the War Cabinet, most likely on the Isle of Wight. Ground nearby had been selected to represent the terrain and they were to practice a night insertion to destroy an enemy HQ, followed by evacuation from a nearby beach. The aim was to persuade Churchill and the War Cabinet that airborne operations had a place as well as seaborne commando raids. The most up to date weapons would be issued and anything the Company needed was to be provided.

The tactics and troops to task had already been laid down and the Company would be split into groups with specialist tasks and equipment. Frost was unhappy about changing the normal company organization, as it reduced flexibility to cater for the inevitable problems that arise on an operation, particularly one involving parachuting at night. He was somewhat confused and frustrated by the inflexible plan forced upon him.

Overnight Frost made his own plan, based upon the requirements in Bromley-Martin's briefing and took it to HQ Airborne Division to see Browning. However, he was away and Bromley-Martin took Frost to see the General Staff Officer Grade 1 (GSO1). Bromley-Martin and Frost both argued their cases, but as a result there was to be no change to the plan. Frost remained troubled and could not fathom the reason for the inflexibility.

Next morning Bromley-Martin returned to Tilshead and saw Frost privately. He bound Frost to secrecy and told him to maintain the cover story with his men, but revealed he would be taking them to France before the end of February to dismantle and return something. If they were to get in and out, he had to comply with the plan laid down as it had been devised to take account of the German defences. If he wanted to lead the raid he had to agree the plan. Frost agreed, while privately maintaining his doubts, but turned his attention to training the Company. Tantalizingly Bromley-Martin said, 'I don't think I should tell you about Private Newman yet.' The cover story worked very well at Tilshead; the Quartermaster of the Glider Pilot Regiment was sufficiently misled that, when he read about the raid in the newspaper, he refused to connect it with C Company.

Lorries were provided with drivers to get them to the various training locations. Once the snow cleared, initial training was carried out at Golden Ball Hill, eight kms southwest of Marlborough near Alton Friars in Wiltshire. The site was similar to Bruneval, but distances between features were different and the slopes less steep. They practiced moving from the imaginary DZ to the objective and then to the mock beach. 9th Field Company RE set up three mock-ups of the target site. They cut

Matching countryside for training purposes was located at Golden Ball Hill, near Alton Friars, Wiltshire.

The 'cliffs' on the southern slopes of Golden Ball Hill at Alton Priors.

'RECTANGLE' on Golden Ball Hill f the simulated *Würzburg* site.

The 'northern cliffs' and evacuation route at Golden Ball Hill overlooking the 'beach'.

Looking towards the simulated DZ RV from the corner of 'RECTANGLE' Golden Ball Hill.

Captain John Ross (back to camera) chatting with four of the Bruneval raiders while training on the beach at Redcliff Point in Dorset on 16 February 1942. Inset: Captain John Ross.

down hedges, built woods, taped out roads and erected tents to simulate buildings. As they were not party to the reason for this huge effort on a bleak and freezing windswept hillside, they were less than enchanted, but the rehearsals were invaluable.

Frost worked them hard. They rarely knew when they'd be in camp and, when they did turn up, the Glider Pilot Regiment staff were alarmed by how much food they ploughed through.

Company Sergeant Major Strachan.

In addition to the intensive training, the 2IC, Captain John Ross, had to deal with the numerous administrative details, including receiving masses of new equipment.

Despite the hectic programme, Frost ensured there was a free twenty-four hour period each week and laid on transport into Salisbury or other nearby towns. Some of the men were pretty wild and their excesses had to be controlled carefully by Company Sergeant Major (CSM) Strachan, who set an excellent example for the NCOs. Some of the wilder elements returned to camp one night from the Tilshead pubs, marching behind an improvised band, the instruments having been 'borrowed' from the local British Legion. On another occasion the room occupied by Sergeants Alex Reid and Jimmy Sharp was burst into by another sergeant brandishing a Sten. He had been involved in some serious drinking and needed some persuasion not to shoot a large cheese held by another man. The mere threat of being returned to Hardwick usually had a salutary effect.

On 7 February the parachute force drove to Thruxton, where they met the RAF crews who would fly them and saw the modification work being carried out on the Whitleys. They also practiced loading their containers (and exit drills from the aircraft. Pickard was away and when he returned later was disappointed that his men were not flying, but soon relaxed. Frost was impressed and Pickard became an instant success with all ranks.

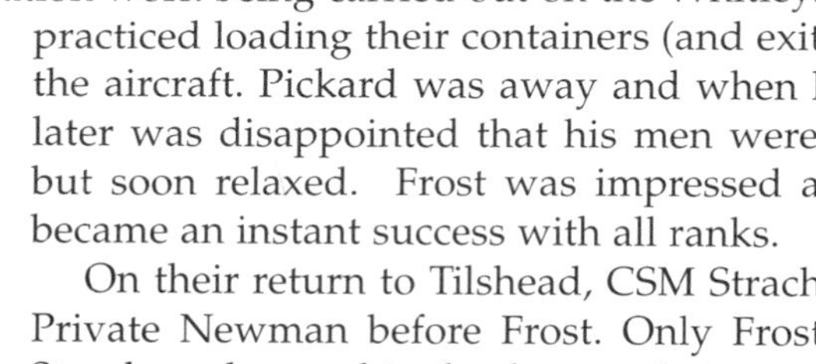

Peter Nagel a few years after the war – his family managed to get out of Germany in the 1930s and he worked in his father's factory in Leicester. He enlisted in the Pioneer Corps in March 1940 and transferred to the Special Operations Executive with the alias Walker.

On their return to Tilshead, CSM Strachan brought Private Newman before Frost. Only Frost, Ross and Strachan knew his background in case he was captured. Newman was actually Peter Nagel, one of 8,000 German and Austrian Jews who served in the British forces as 'His Majesty's Most Loyal Enemy Aliens'. When a German speaker was required for the raid, Nagel was chosen and given the identity of a soldier named Newman who had deserted before the war. If captured his details would tally with the Red Cross. Frost noted his toughness, intelligence, humour and language skills, but

Loading containers prior to a drop.

felt uneasy about 'having a Hun on the strength'.

On 9 February the parachute force, consisting at that time of eight officers and 148 other ranks, travelled by train to the Combined Operations Training Centre at Inveraray on Loch Fyne in Scotland. They removed their parachute wings en route as a security measure. At Inveraray they lived aboard HMS *Prins Albert*, which was very civilised after Tilshead. The main reason to be there was to practice embarking on the landing craft that would evacuate them after the raid. They learned quickly that this was hazardous and difficult work at night. The landing craft found it difficult to locate them on shore and whatever the state of the tide it always seemed to be wrong for what they wanted to do. They did not manage a single successful night embarkation, but everyone enjoyed the weather, the change of

Inveraray on Loch Fyne with various Combined Operations vessels moored offshore.

scenery and a new experience.

The men from No.12 Commando, who would provide fire support from the landing craft during the evacuation, had arrived at Inveraray on 8 February. On 12 February, Lieutenant A S Baker and twenty medics joined from 181st Airlanding Field Ambulance RAMC, based at Chilton Foliat near Hungerford in Wiltshire. On the raid, the medics would sail part of the way on HMS *Prins Albert*, before transferring two to each ALC and one to each LCS to provide medical support to the returning paratroopers. As there was no room for medics within the

With brand new Stens, but without parachute wings, raiders board an ALC from the main deck of HMS *Prins Albert*, prior to a beach evacuation exercise.

The raiders settle in the ALC prior to being lowered. Note the variety of weaponry and a few RE cap badges amongst the Scottish headwear. The sandbags are for the fire support teams to rest their weapons.

Disembarking on a beach near Inveraray.

Embarkation practice always resulted in freezing cold wet feet. Note the fire support team, two soldiers with Brens fitted with 100 rounds pan magazine and a third with a Boys Anti-Tank Rifle pointing forward on the left.

parachute force, twelve men (four in each group) were given extra medical training and issued with morphine and bandages. In addition all officers were issued with five tubes of morphine.

One night Frost was asked to make his men scarce next day, as the ship was being visited by Mountbatten. Next morning while they were training ashore, the ship's whistle blew, the ALCs were seen coming for them and urgent messages were received over the 38 Sets telling Frost that Mountbatten wanted to see them immediately. On board Mountbatten addressed everyone. It was the first the Navy knew that the Pongos (soldiers) were paratroopers or that they were all about to take part in a raid together, although the destination and purpose were not mentioned. Mountbatten stressed that inter-service cooperation was essential. As a result of the revelations the skipper of HMS *Prins Albert* cancelled all leave and outgoing mail until after the operation.

Privately Mountbatten asked Frost if he had any concerns. Frost was unhappy about Private Newman, so Mountbatten subjected him to a barrage of questions in fluent German. Newman answered quietly and smoothly, they shook hands and he was dismissed. Mountbatten said to Frost, 'Take him along; you won't regret it for he is bound to be very useful. I judge him to be brave and intelligent. After all, he risks far more than you do and of course he would never have been attached to you if he had not passed security on every count.' Newman recalled the Admiral was charming.

Next day HMS *Prins Albert* steamed to Gourock, from where the paratroopers returned by train to Tilshead, arriving on 14 February. With the medical and fire support parties on board, HMS *Prins Albert* then steamed for Portland, arriving on 15 February, to prepare for further exercises with Frost's men.

On 15 February, the parachute force carried out aircraft drills with 51 Squadron in the morning, followed by a practice parachute drop watched by Browning in the afternoon. The aircrews had not dropped live paratroopers before and with lots of delay and confusion on the airfield, Frost judged the exercise was a shambles. It wasn't until late in the day that the drop took place onto rock hard ground in front of HQ Airborne Division at Syrencot House near Netheravon. The containers were dropped in this exercise and most deployed correctly, but some adjustments were required. Frost noted that Sergeant Grieve's

Syrencot House on the River Avon, three kms south of Netheravon airfield, housed HQ Airborne Division. Later it was the HQ of 6th Airborne Division prior to the invasion of Normandy.

stick deplaned very quickly and resolved that the rest had to reach this standard.

During the preparations for the jump, every man was weighed so the centre of gravity of the aircraft could be maintained. Frost at six feet was the heaviest in the Company by almost a stone. In his stick he accounted for fifteen stones of the total weight of 130 stones. Weighing every man was not just procedural routine; the troops had it drummed into them that unless they adopted their allocated take off position the alternative was almost certainly a crash. For take off they all had to be forward of the exit hatch, but in the air they could spread out.

Equipment was no problem. Ross asked for nine Bren Guns and received eighteen brand new ones next day. Anything they needed turned up – Colt .45 pistols, watches, torches, binoculars, boots, compasses, escape kits and rations, silk gloves, sleeping bags, white snow suits – while the rest of the Army was having a pretty lean time of it. Things they had not ordered also turned up – anti-tank mines, mine detectors and the new and highly unreliable Sten Guns, which had to be trained with from scratch. Four of the new 38 Set radios appeared for Company HQ and the three groups, and two 18 Sets to contact the Navy.

In the cellars of Danesfield House at Medmenham in

Large-scale model of the area around Bruneval. RECTANGLE is close to the cliffs in the centre with the ravine leading to the beach above it.

Sten Gun Mk.II (designed by Shepherd and Turpin and produced by Enfield, hence Sten). Manufacturing was simple, requiring minimal machining and early versions often required the users to file down rough edges to ensure they didn't jam. Stens worked on the blowback principle, with the bolt to the rear (open bolt) until released by the trigger. When the bolt flew forward it picked up a round from the 32 round box magazine, chambered it and fired it in one movement. Reloading used the recoil energy; very simple but also very dangerous once the safety catch was released.

Buckinghamshire, the RAF CIU's workshop built a number of models of Bruneval from air photographs and blown up French maps. Everything was to scale – houses, radars, pillboxes, fences, gates etc. Every man became very familiar with the layout and they received last minute updates on the defences, even the names of some of the German garrison were known.

Beach evacuation exercises followed on the Dorset coast. Three sites were considered suitable; in priority order these were:

Arish Mell Cove – east of Lulworth in the tank training area.

The beach half a mile east of Redcliff Point near Osmington.

Bowleaze Cove near Weymouth – it does not appear to have been used.

Troops from 113 Infantry Brigade (38th Division, V Corps,

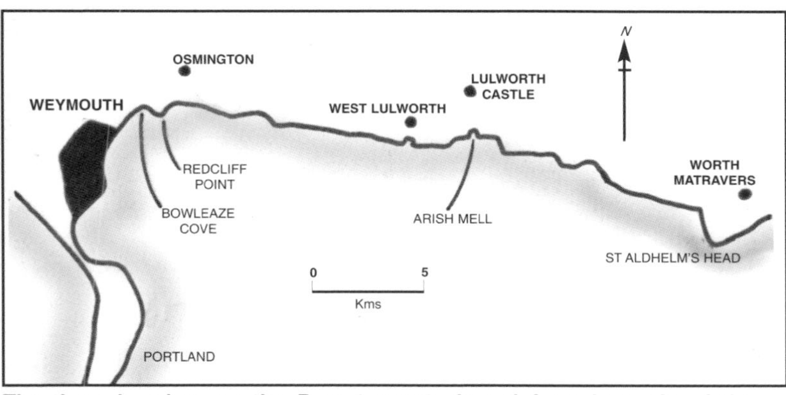

The three beaches on the Dorset coast cleared for rehearsals of the operation. Arish Mell was very close to TRE Worth.

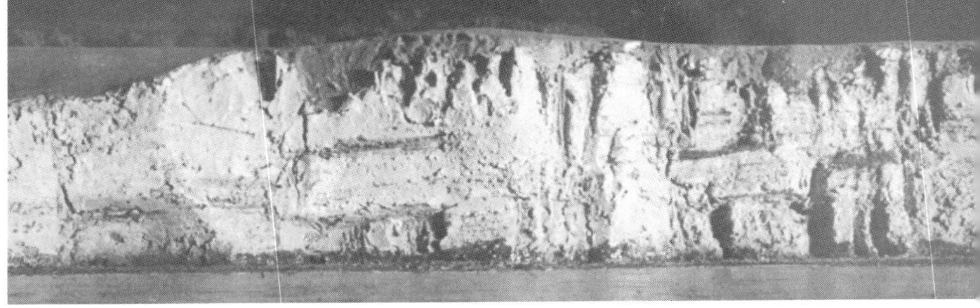

Model of the cliffs as they would appear in moonlight for the pilots to familiarise themselves with the key landmarks. RECTANGLE is top left and LONE HOUSE top right.

Detailed model of LONE HOUSE and HENRY for the assault party. Frost burst in through the main door on the left while others entered through the windows overlooking the terrace on the right. The terrace and cellars beneath it are all that remain today.

Southern Command) cleared the beaches sufficiently of mines, scaffolding and wire to allow the training to go ahead. The exercises started at Redcliff Point on 16 February and were filmed, but the night rehearsal was cancelled due to bad weather and C Company returned to Tilshead.

On 17 February there was a night exercise with air and naval forces at Arish Mell, but the weather turned and the ground was frozen. The troops waited on a mock DZ for 51 Squadron to drop their containers, before launching a mock attack followed by the move to the beach at Arish Mell for evacuation. Group Captain Norman intended this exercise to be a full rehearsal for his crews less the paratroopers. They used Oxford as the initial RV and

ALCs approach the beach near Redcliff Point at Osmington on 16 February 1942.

The beach and cliffs at Redcliff Point are unchanged 70 years on. Weymouth is in the distance.

Above: One of the hazards was the ALC broaching on the shore and becoming stuck on a falling tide.

Inset left: The same scene in October 2010.

Below: Raiders tumbling down the cliffs to meet an ALC.

Boarding an ALC in daylight was a much simpler proposition than in the dark - behind are cleared anti-invasion defences.

The same beach in October 2010.

Swanage as the landfall. Flying along the ridge of downs westwards over Corfe Castle they were to drop the containers into a semi-circular field just south of Lulworth Castle and the B3070. To ensure the containers dropped correctly the loadmasters in the rear of the aircraft waited for the green light then counted, '1000, 2000, 3000, 4000, 5000', to simulate the first five paratroopers leaving the aircraft, before releasing them.

The whole exercise was a shambles. Most containers dropped in the wrong place, the troops got lost in a real minefield and the ALCs arrived at the wrong beach. The paratroopers stayed that night at the Armoured Fighting Vehicle Gunnery School at West Lulworth.

On 18 February the weather didn't allow aircraft to be used, but the troops went through their part of the operation. The Navy also cancelled due to bad weather. The troops stayed overnight at Lulworth again. Poor progress with the evacuation training did nothing to inspire confidence in the Royal Navy's ability to bring them home.

The troops returned to Tilshead on 19 February and had a

Two ALCs being towed in tandem by a MGB.

lecture on escaping by MI9 (set up to assist prisoners of war (POW) to escape). Next day they had demonstrations of crossing wire obstacles by No.3 Commando. As a result of the disastrous

exercises in Dorset, the Navy demanded a final evacuation rehearsal. By then HMS *Prins Albert* had moved into the Solent in preparation for the raid. The exercise took place that night on Southampton Water, as the weather outside was too windy and rough.

The troops, with all their kit and a trolley loaded with a boulder, made a silent withdrawal to the beach. For once contact was established with the Navy on the 18 Sets and the ALCs

Some of these raiders have had a soaking and seem amused as they watch their comrades getting the same treatment. Note the Fairburn-Sykes fighting knife scabbards poking out from under some smocks.

arrived at the right place at 2015. They were well offshore and called the paratroopers to wade out. Frost decided there was no point risking the weapons and trolley, which were left on shore under guard. The water was icy cold and they waded out to the top of their thighs. With the paratroopers aboard, the ALCs went astern, but a miscalculation with the tides meant they grounded

Scene of the final evacuation exercise at Hamble on Southampton Water.

fifty metres offshore and could not be shifted despite the efforts of all the troops in the water trying to push them off. With a falling tide they were stuck until it turned again. The troops gave up, waded ashore and were driven back to Tilshead, cold and wet.

The next three days were spent collecting kit, packing containers, practicing again and again the role of each party and attacking pillboxes by day and night. They spent as long as possible studying the models and air photographs.

51 Squadron also trained hard for the raid, adapting from dropping bombs at high level to paratroopers at just over 100 metres. They dropped practice dummies, aiming at white strips on the ground. They navigated 130 kms at low level to locate two specific fields and drop a dummy on each, on time and without a preliminary circuit. They also made low approaches to DZs to drop containers.

These were the days before paratroopers jumped with their kit. Weapons and equipment were carried in containers dropped from the aircraft bomb bay and the ideal was for them to land in the middle of the stick of paratroopers. To achieve this required some innovation. An intercom plug attached to the fifth paratrooper's static line interrupted the bomb release circuit. When he exited the aircraft the plug was pulled out, completing the circuit and releasing the containers. The sixth jumper had to wait an extra second to allow the containers to fall clear. In case the plug came out prematurely, the circuit was wired so it would not operate until the green light came on. At worst the containers would fall at the beginning of the stick rather than in the middle.

The Airborne Forces Experimental Establishment (AFEE) at Ringway produced new containers at short notice. They were marked with white bands to identify the group they belonged to and fitted with coloured lights to identify the contents. The lights illuminated on impact and were visible up to 100 metres to make identification on the DZ easier. The packing of each container was worked out precisely to ensure the centre of gravity was maintained. The containers were marked as follows:

Bands

1 – NELSON.
2 – HARDY and JELLICOE.
3 – DRAKE.
4 – RODNEY.

Lights

Red – weapons.
Green – signals.
Purple – sappers.
Yellow – trolleys.

On 12 February, Pickard flew Norman on a high level reconnaissance over Bruneval in his Whitley. Visibility was poor, but they saw the main features and noted Cap d'Antifer lighthouse was working on reduced brilliance.

Norman intended there be much more joint training between aircrew and paratroopers than actually occurred. He envisaged a series of exercises growing in complexity, starting with dropping containers to the paratroopers on the ground prior to them carrying out dry runs of their tasks. Next would follow two full daylight and night rehearsals. Due to adverse weather and the need to practice the beach evacuation again, no night drops took place and only one day drop.

Press representatives were included with the naval and air forces. One flew in one of the 51 Squadron aircraft and three

Cap d'Antifer lighthouse with earth-covered German defences on the edge of the cliff, including the base of a *Freya* radar on the left. The bunker directly below the lighthouse is Stand 1 on the tour of the battlefield.

went with the naval force, two in the landing craft, but they were not allowed to land. Their reports were subject to censorship by HQ Combined Operations.

The section of sappers included in the parachute force underwent specialist training. Every man learned the role of every other in case of casualties and there was a 30% reserve of trained manpower. Early on, it was realised they had insufficient expertise to identify the important components to be brought back.

Flight Sergeant Charles Cox – before the war he was a cinema projectionist and radio ham. Before being selected for the operation he had never been in a ship or aircraft before.

Don Preist, the TRE radar expert with a RAFVR commission as a Flight Lieutenant, volunteered for parachute training to accompany the parachute force. However, he knew too much about British radar to be allowed to jump with the main force. Instead, if conditions allowed, he would go ashore from a landing craft and dash to the *Würzburg* to make a technical assessment.

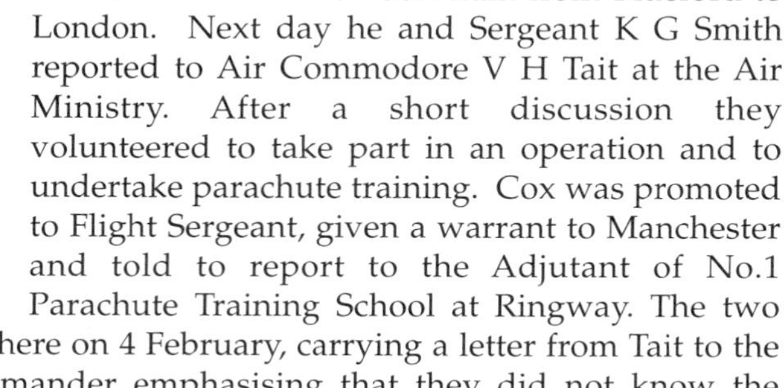

Someone else, with less knowledge of British radar secrets, was required to accompany the parachute force. On 1 February, RAF Sergeant C W H Cox based at Hartland Point Chain Home Low station in Devon, was handed a rail warrant and told to catch the noon train from Bideford to London. Next day he and Sergeant K G Smith reported to Air Commodore V H Tait at the Air Ministry. After a short discussion they volunteered to take part in an operation and to undertake parachute training. Cox was promoted to Flight Sergeant, given a warrant to Manchester and told to report to the Adjutant of No.1 Parachute Training School at Ringway. The two proceeded there on 4 February, carrying a letter from Tait to the station commander emphasising that they did not know the details of the duties they would be employed upon.

On the second balloon jump Smith tore a leg muscle and soon after fell ill. After four days of bad weather Cox carried out his first 'singles' drop (one paratrooper dropped on each pass over the DZ), from a Whitley. Two multiple jumps, in which a number of paratroopers dropped in succession, were followed by a night jump from a balloon on 14 February. Having been awarded his wings, Cox arrived at Netheravon then Tilshead on the 15th, just

ABBEY 3411
Extn. 5542....

[Any] communications on the [s]ubject of this letter should [be] addressed to :—
[T]HE UNDER SECRETARY [O]F STATE, AIR MINISTRY, [a]nd the following number [q]uoted :—

/D. of R.

CONFIDENTIAL.

AIR MINISTRY,
LONDON, S.W.1.

4th February, 1942.

Group Captain Hervey,
Royal Air Force Station,
Ringway.

This letter will be delivered to you by 955754 Flight Sergeant Cox, C.W.H. who, in company with 915291 Sergeant Smith K.G., will be reporting to you. They are reporting to you under arrangements made with Captain Hughes Hallett and Major-General Browning. I understand that you have full knowledge of the proposed employment of these two N.C.O's and will arrange all details as to any necessary training, and for their accommodation, pay, rationing, etc.

2. These two N.C.O's are as yet unacquainted with the duties on which it is proposed they should be employed or the training that will be required to prepare them for carrying out such duties. If there are any further details or you require information regarding these N.C.O's, will you please communicate direct with me at this address.

V. H. Tait.
Air Commodore,
Director of Radio.

S 5/2/[illegible]

Air Commodore Tait's letter to Group Captain Hervey at Ringway.

in time to join the paratroopers on their way to Thruxton to practice emplaning. His account says there was no jumping, but perhaps he meant he did not jump as it is clear from reliable sources that there was a drop at Syrencot House late in the day. His name does not appear on the manifests.

CSM Strachan briefed Cox about the exercise, but by then Cox knew sufficient to know it was not an exercise. He could hardly understand the Jocks in C Company, but undertook a

Mk.II gun-laying radar similar to the one the dismantling party trained with.

week of physical training, route marches, unarmed combat and night patrolling with them. He described the fortnight before the raid as boring, but perhaps that was with tongue in cheek.

Cox is often described as a radar expert. In reality he was a highly skilled radar technician. The story that the paratroopers were under orders to shoot him, if his capture looked likely, is a myth. It was intended originally to have two RAF radar NCOs in case one was incapacitated or did not arrive, but with Sergeant Smith injured in training it was decided that Cox and Lieutenant Vernon RE were capable between them of handling any radar they found. Cox's job was to locate the *Würzburg*, photograph it and oversee the disassembly for transportation back to Britain.

Sir Basil Schonland - a South African who served in the RE Signal Service in France 1915-18 and was wounded at Arras. Between the wars he was a prominent physicist with posts at Cambridge, Cape Town and Witwatersrand Universities. He was Superintendent of the AORG 1941-44, then scientific adviser to Montgomery with 21st Army Group. Post-war he was first Chancellor of Rhodes University, Director of the Atomic Energy Research Establishment at Harwell and later Director of the research group of the UK Atomic Energy Authority. He was knighted in 1960.

Cox worked closely with the sappers. A mobile gun laying radar arrived and Cox instructed them on what it was and how it worked. On 19 February, Lieutenant Colonel Sir Basil Schonland, Superintendent of the Army Operational Research Group (AORG) of the Air Defence Research and Development Establishment at Richmond, Surrey, trained the sappers on how to dismantle it, which they did repeatedly. Schonland then set up a mock-up of what he thought a German radar station might look like and tested them to see which components they would select and which of lesser importance they would leave behind.

The sappers were also instructed in how to avoid electrocuting themselves. They practiced fusing and arming anti-tank mines and using the Polish mine detector. Practice in the use of burglary tools and small explosive charges was particularly popular and the sappers proved quite good at these aspects. They also trained with the infantry on the ranges, PT, map reading, night work and tactical exercises. Lieutenant Vernon and Corporal Day were taught basic flash photography by Flight Lieutenant May at RAF Old Sarum near Salisbury, but the training was rushed.

On 20 February, Cox and Vernon were separately sent on two days leave and told to report to the Air Ministry on the afternoon of the second day. Cox squeezed in a night at home in Wisbech. They were surprised to see each other at the Air Ministry, where R V Jones and Don Preist interviewed them. A Frenchman in British uniform sitting between them didn't say much. The importance of the mission and what was required was emphasised. They were also briefed on various interrogation techniques they may encounter if captured and how to contact the Resistance if left behind. Jones warned Cox to beware the kindly approach by an interrogator; Cox reckoned he could withstand a lot of kindness.

Chapter Seven

INSERTION BY PARACHUTE

THE OPTIMUM requirements for the operation were a full moon for visibility and a rising tide to ensure the ALCs would not become stuck on the shore. This limited the period to 23 – 26 February. Wind over Force 3 would cause too much swell to lower the landing craft or allow embarkation from the beach.

Each day the troops packed their equipment, had a good lunch and braced themselves for action. Each evening the operation was cancelled because weather conditions were unsuitable. Frost expected the operation to be abandoned and the force sent on leave before trying again at the end of March. Only Strachan remained optimistic. On 27 February, the day it should have been cancelled, visibility was reasonable and the wind dropped. The Meteorological Officer at Tangmere, Flight Lieutenant Crichton-Miller, forecast ideal conditions for the coming night; no wind or swell, bright moonlight, very light haze and visibility up to six kilometres.

Cook rang the Flag Lieutenant and asked to see the Commander-in-Chief urgently. Admiral James had been bombed out of this office in Portsmouth and was working from Nelson's cabin on HMS *Victory*. Cook made the case to go that night; although outside the ideal period, the weather would be good and keeping security for another month didn't bear thinking about. James pointed out the tide would be falling, but Cook showed him a pre-war postcard of a woman standing in the water close to the shore. It was apparent that the beach shelved more steeply than had been anticipated and limited the risk of the landing craft becoming stuck.

At 1507, Commander-in-Chief Portsmouth sent out the signal, 'Carry out Operation BITING tonight 27 February.' Major General Browning himself brought the news to Frost at Tilshead and wished them all luck. Mountbatten signaled, 'Operation Biting – to all hands – good luck. Bite-em-hard.'

The operation was controlled from Commander-in-Chief Portsmouth's Operations Room at Fort Wallington, one of the Palmerston Folly forts built around Portsmouth in the 1860-70s.

Fort Wallington from the air prior to the majority of it being demolished and the land used for an industrial estate.

Group Captain Norman and Lieutenant Colonel A G Walsh, GSO1 HQ Airborne Division, were there throughout.

Cook's naval force weighed anchor at 1645 and passed the Portsmouth boom at 1712. Cook had one other regular naval officer, the rest of the force being reservists. Carrying its eight landing craft, HMS *Prins Albert* was followed by five MGBs and two escorting destroyers. The weather was perfect. They took a last fix on the Isle of Wight and steered by dead reckoning to arrive at the EA5 Rescue Float at 1925 and then on to a point 32 kilometres short of Bruneval by 2215. They arrived there early at 2147 and the landing craft were deployed from HMS *Prins Albert* in record time (only two and half minutes) at 2152. Cook transferred to SLC2 to be closer to the beach. Accompanied by the MGBs they set off in the moonlight for a point three miles short of the beach.

Modern comparison of the picture opposite.

HMS *Prins Albert* flashed a message of good speed and turned for home with the escorts, as they were too large to go unnoticed as the force closed the French coast. On the way back they behaved as if laying mines in case the Germans were plotting them on radar. HMS *Prins Albert* anchored off Spithead at 0241 next morning to await the return of its ALCs.

SLC2 developed engine trouble twenty-seven kilometres from Bruneval and was taken in tow by a MGB. The flotilla engineering officer on HMS *Prins Albert*, Lieutenant C W J Coles,

pre-war postcard of the beach at Bruneval showing how steeply it shelved from the igh water line.

Inset left: A close up from the same postcard shows more clearly the steepness of the fall – people a few metres offshore are already up to their waist.

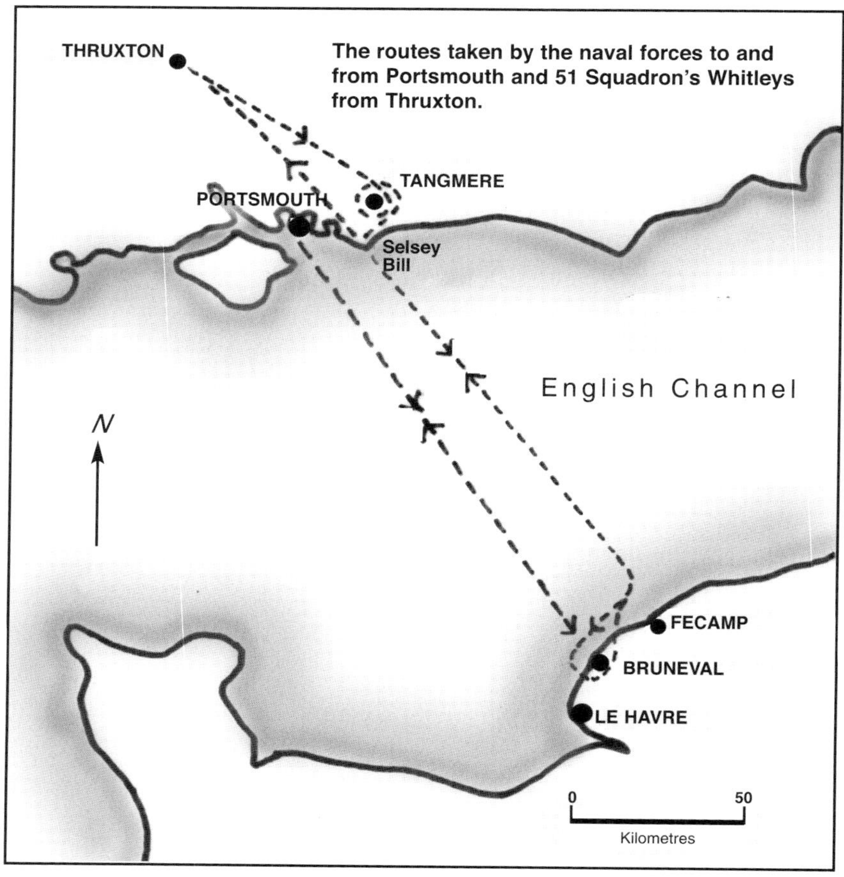

had volunteered to accompany the boats in case of breakdowns. He worked in very difficult cramped circumstances with little light and the craft being constantly snatched by the towing line, but completed the repairs in time for the craft to take part in the evacuation.

At 2306 they couldn't believe their luck as the Cap d'Antifer lighthouse gave a few flashes, which allowed them to plot an accurate fix. It was only later they realised the significance of the light being switched on. The boats were five kilometres offshore at 0023, where they were scheduled to wait, but Cook decided to push on to three kilometres offshore, which was to prove fortuitous. They settled down to wait, some anchoring to maintain their positions.

At 1900 at Bruneval the *Würzburg* night shift of eight men

came on duty expecting to be relieved at 0800 next morning. During the night they rotated duties, with two manning the radar and one in the lookout post nearby equipped with a French light machine-gun, binoculars and a telephone linked to the coastal defence reporting centre at Le Havre. The remainder slept in a nearby dugout.

At the beach house (Stella Maris), three men were on sentry duty at one time, while another manned the telephone to take messages, alert the sergeant if required and wake the next sentry in good time. It was a familiar routine and nothing seemed unusual that night. At 2020 one of the young German soldiers came off sentry duty, took off his equipment and boots and went to sleep. Little did he suspect in a few hours he would be on his way to England.

Final RAF reconnaissance flights flew over the area. At dusk a Spitfire of 92 Squadron checked the sea state along the coast for sixty-five kilometres north and east of Le Havre. Between 2000 and 2100 a Havoc of 23 Squadron flew along the coast near the objective to report on visibility and suitability for parachute operations. This aircraft also measured the barometric pressure at Bruneval, so the Whitley crews could set their altimeters accurately for the drop. The reconnaissance aircraft had to land by 2115 to allow time to pass their information to Thruxton prior to take-off.

At Tilshead the final preparations were by now very familiar. At 1400 the containers were sent to Thruxton to arrive by 1500. Cox heard the mission was on at 1700, about the time they were scheduled to have a last hot meal. At 1900 they received French money and a French handkerchief map between two. Once everything had been checked, Frost gave the men a final talk urging them to uphold the worthy names of their regiments. Then to the sound of the bagpipes, they boarded five lorries and

Douglas Havoc light bomber and night fighter – the RAF called them Bostons in the bomber role.

set off for Thruxton at 1930 arriving at 2030.

Having packed his men off, Frost stayed at Tilshead to have a meal with his host officers of the Glider Pilot Regiment. He said nothing about the mission and afterwards changed into his parachuting gear. On the way out he looked into the mess and grinned at the pilots dozing in front of the fire. He struggled into the back of a staff car with his batman and was driven to the airfield.

While the men waited in three blacked out Nissen huts around the perimeter, Frost, Ross and Strachan passed around the groups chatting and joking with them as they checked their gear. Some were singing and drinking tea laced with rum. Cox recalls it was at this time that Frost revealed where their target was, gave them the password 'Biting' and told them there was snow on the ground in France.

Cox described the dramatic atmosphere inside the huts with camouflaged parachutes laid out on the floor. Each man chose his own, silently praying the lass who packed it had done it properly. As fitting and checking went on they munched huge corned beef sandwiches and drank more rum laced tea.

Just before 2200 Frost's men marched around the perimeter track to the sound of their regimental marches played on the bagpipes by Private Ewing, who was going on the raid, but left his pipes behind. Each stick peeled off as they reached their aircraft. To save space the Elsan toilets had been removed and the troops were advised to relieve themselves before boarding.

Just before take off, Frost was called to the telephone in the control vehicle, where Pickard had been waiting to receive any changes of plan from Portsmouth. Norman told him the reconnaissance flights had just returned. The sea was calm and visibility was good, but France was covered in snow and the air defences appeared to be alert. The snowsuits were at Tilshead and it was too late to return for them, but on reflection Frost thought it better to go without to aid recognition in the dark. All he said to Pickard was, 'Damn we could have worn our whites!'

Pickard took Frost to one side just before they boarded and told him, 'I feel like a bloody murderer!' However, the sight of him calmly puffing his pipe, and the rest of his crews relaxed but professional, was reassuring for Frost and his men. They boarded the twelve Whitleys (the two reserve aircraft were not required) and the first took off at 2215, the last 18½ minutes later.

As Pickard's aircraft left the ground there was a loud cheer from his passengers. When the last aircraft was airborne, the Thruxton ground controller signaled Commander-in-Chief Portsmouth, 'Walnut Twelve', to indicate all planes were heading for France. The aircraft settled into three groups of four, separated by five minutes. Radios were only to be used in emergency.

The flight was just over two hours. The aircraft first flew to Tangmere beacon with Pickard's aircraft arriving dead on schedule. He had allowed half an hour for unforeseen problems, so although this part of the flight was only thirty minutes they flew around to make it last one hour. At 2315 Pickard fired the colour of the day and was the first to leave the British coast at Selsey Bill. Coincidentally as they flew towards France, agent Remy was flying north in a Lysander for a meeting in London, having been picked up in a field about eighty kilometres east of Bruneval.

Halfway over the Channel the Whitleys ran into the expected 9/10ths cloud cover at 300 metres and came down to fly 15-180 metres above the waves. The men in the rear of the Whitleys were wrapped in sleeping bags and had silk gloves and flasks of rum-laced tea against the cold, but sitting on the ribbed floor and unable to move around was still uncomfortable. In Pickard's aircraft there was much singing, including 'Annie Laurie', 'Lulu' and the song of parachute troops, 'Come and sit by my side if you love me', to the tune of 'Red River Valley'. The words of the printable version are:

Come and sit by my side if you love me,
Do not hasten to bid me adieu,
Just remember the poor parachutist,
And the job he is trying to do.

Westland Lysander army co-operation and liaison raft had an exceptionally short take off and landing ability and was able to fly very slowly without lling, making it ideal for covert operations picking and dropping off agents in occupied Europe.

When the red light goes on we are ready,
For the sergeant to shout 'Number One',
Though we sit in the plane close together,
We all tumble out one by one.

When we're coming in for a landing,
Just remember your sergeant's advice,
Keep your feet and your knees close together,
And you'll land on the ground very nice.

When we land in one certain country,
There's a job we'll do very well,
We'll fire Göring and old Adolf Hitler,
And all of those bastards as well.

So come stand by the bar with your glasses,
Drink a toast to the men of the sky,
Drink a toast to the men dead already,
Three cheers for the next man to die!

Cox gave a solo rendition of 'The Rose of Tralee' and 'Because'. Others played pontoon, including Corporal Stewart who won handsomely as usual; he told the others they were in luck if he was hit. Although most had relieved themselves on the airfield just before embarking, the effects of lots of tea combined with the cold began to be felt.

The *Freya* at Bruneval picked up the Whitleys when they were seventy-five kilometres away. When they were sixty kilometres out the *Würzburg* was alerted so it could be warmed up; the display equipment took two minutes to become visible. The operators calibrated on a known reflection on a bearing of 45 degrees about seven kilometres away near Étretat. Once calibrated the operator swung onto the bearing the *Freya* station announced through a loudspeaker. The operator moved the dish left and right and up and down by rotating handles until he gained maximum readings for the range and altitude of the target, which he passed to his control HQ by telephone. The first report was sent at 2355 when the aircraft were twenty-nine kilometres away and was updated every three kilometres. The *Würzburg* saw them change course at Fecamp and the speed indicated a bomber force heading directly for them. The radar was switched off and the crew dived for the dugout shelters. Throughout the German defences men were being alerted, as it was realized that something unusual was developing.

About thirty minutes from the DZ, the aircrews alerted the paratroopers who began to get out of their bags, fixed their static lines to the fastening wire and prepared to jump. Cox's stick sensibly stayed in their bags another fifteen minutes, then they were passed forward for stowage, static lines were checked and a flask of rum was passed around a few times.

Landfall on the French coast was at Fecamp, sixteen kilometres north of Bruneval. About one and a half kilometres offshore the aircraft circled to get into formation. Then they banked to starboard and flew south parallel with the coast and 800 metres to seaward at a height of 300-460 metres. This allowed the crews to identify landmarks and get an accurate fix. Only aircraft Q was uncertain of its position and returned to Fecamp to make another run; as a result it was nineteen minutes late over the DZ. The Cap d'Antifer lighthouse and RECTANGLE were particularly clear. All except the first two

A trainee paratrooper about to jump from a Whitley – the cramped conditions are evident.

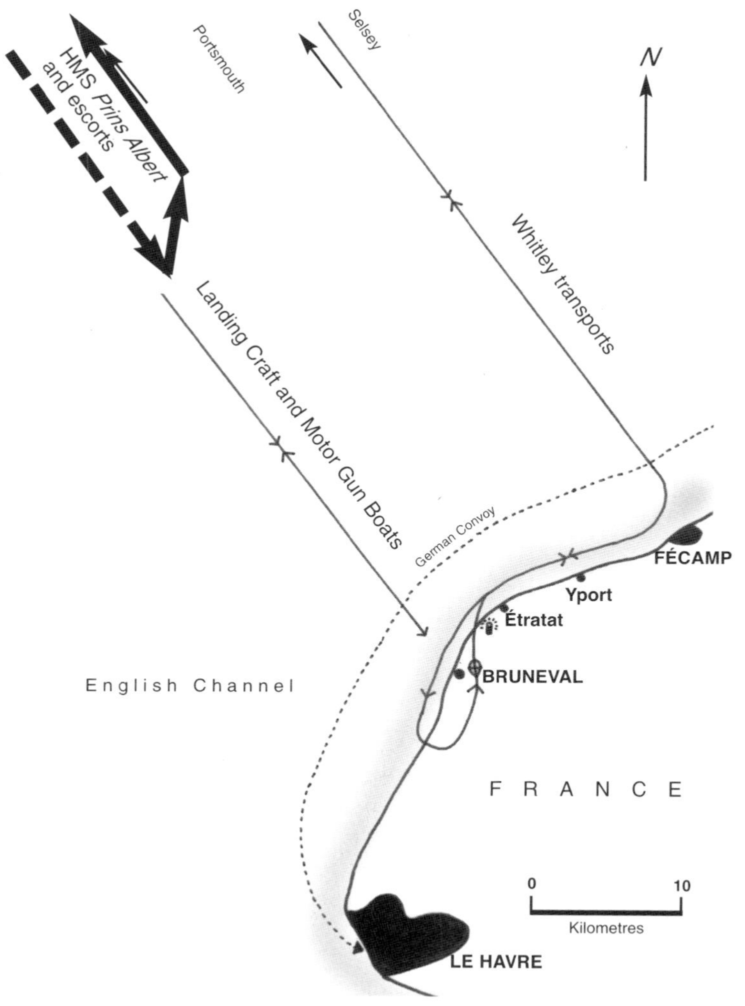

aircraft ran into accurate fire from four flak ships off Yport. Three aircraft were hit, but no serious damage was sustained and there were no casualties. All except the first aircraft experienced more flak from two positions near the coast; the rear gunner of aircraft Y temporarily silenced one of these positions.

Before the raid, No.4 Group of Bomber Command had carried out missions to accustom the Germans to aircraft crossing the coast at low level close to Bruneval. It was hoped on the night of the raid they would suspect nothing different. Commencing on the night of 17/18 February intruder raids in the Paris area crossed the coast between Le Havre and the Somme estuary, but raids on Le Havre itself on four nights between 31 January and 15 February seem to have been unconnected with the Bruneval Raid. Leaflet flights over unspecified parts of France on six nights between 16 and 25 February are likely to have been part of the deception as were intruder missions by Fighter Command night fighters.

Bomber Command was unable to carry out a diversion on the night of the raid due to weather (probably low cloud). At short notice, two Havocs from Fighter Command's 23 Squadron, which at the time was mainly involved in shipping protection and intruder missions, carried out a diversion over an airfield and railway marshalling yard southeast of Le Havre. The defences were on full alert, expecting the intrusion to develop into a heavy bombing raid, but it was sufficient to deflect the attention of night-fighters away from the incoming Whitleys. The searchlights and tracer fire around Le Havre were clearly visible to the Whitleys and the naval force approaching Bruneval.

As the Whitleys passed RECTANGLE the signal for actions stations was given; six minutes to the drop. Below them the

Cramped cockpit of a Whitley bomber, looking forward from the navigator's position.

naval force saw several aircraft pass overhead and gave them a big cheer. There was an icy blast through the hole in the aircraft floor when the hatch was removed. They saw the calm sea in the moonlight then the coast passed below and they were over snow-covered land. The turn over the land took place five kilometres south of the DZ. The aircraft banked to port gradually climbing and when about 500 metres inland banked to port again to bring them onto a line that would take them over the DZ. They reduced altitude to just over 100 metres above ground level and throttled back to 160 kilometres per hour.

Cox saw various colours of tracer in the sky as they crossed the coast and heard the rear gunner responding. Then all attention was on the red and green lights. The first man in each stick was sitting on the aircraft floor next to the hatch. The red light went on when the aircraft was 500 metres south of the east-west road in Bruneval leading to the beach. At this the first man swung his legs through the hole into the buffeting slipstream. The aircraft continued another fifteen seconds (700 metres) until 200 metres north of the road when the green light went on, to land the first man on the forward edge of the DZ. The first aircraft was over the drop point seventy-five seconds early, just after 0013, the second was forty-five seconds early and the remaining two aircraft in the first group were dead on time at 0015.

Two aircraft in the first group (piloted by Pickard and Sergeant Pohe) mistook their landmarks. These aircraft carried the sections commanded by Lieutenant Charteris and Sergeant Grieve. Charteris was in Pickard's aircraft as it took evasive action due to flak, which he described sounding like a man hammering a sheet of tin. Below him he could see every house, tree and fence in the clear moonlight. These two aircraft dropped their sticks two kilometres south of the DZ at the head of Val aux Chats near the hamlet of l'Enfer. Despite this the other aircraft arrived over the correct DZ to drop their sticks. The rear gunners counted the parachutes to ensure all paratroopers and containers had dropped correctly.

Frost says he was first out in his stick. He was bursting due to the tea and angry with himself for not holding back on liquids before setting out. He swore he'd not be caught out again. Out he went, quickly followed by the others. Frost logged the main points from the models, which were exactly as he remembered. It took about 10 seconds to reach the snow-covered ground,

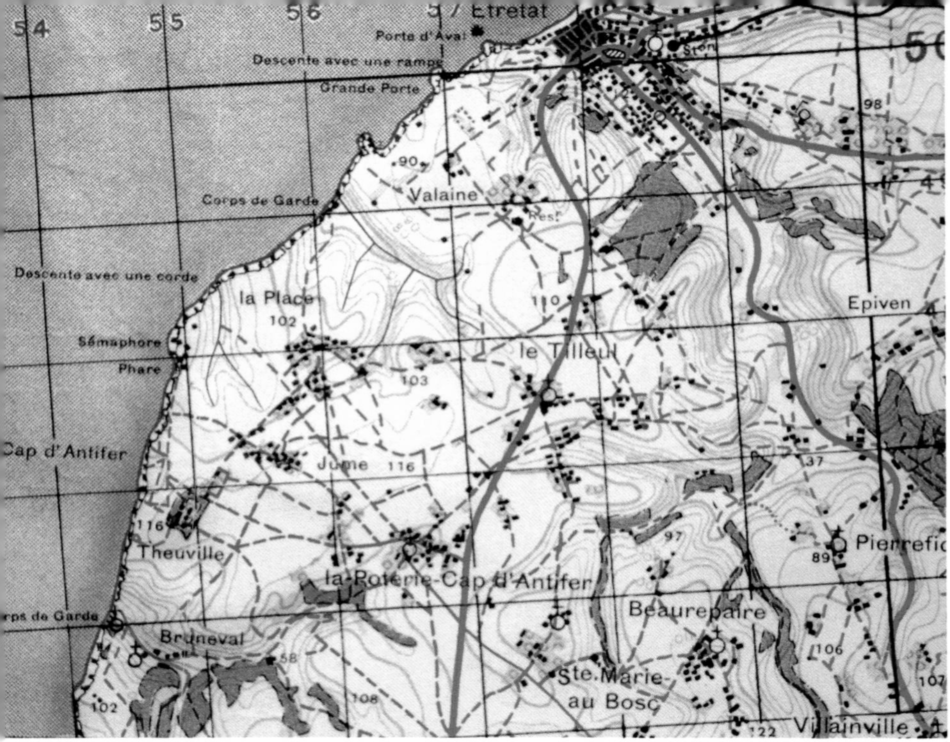

A wartime French map of the area of the raid.

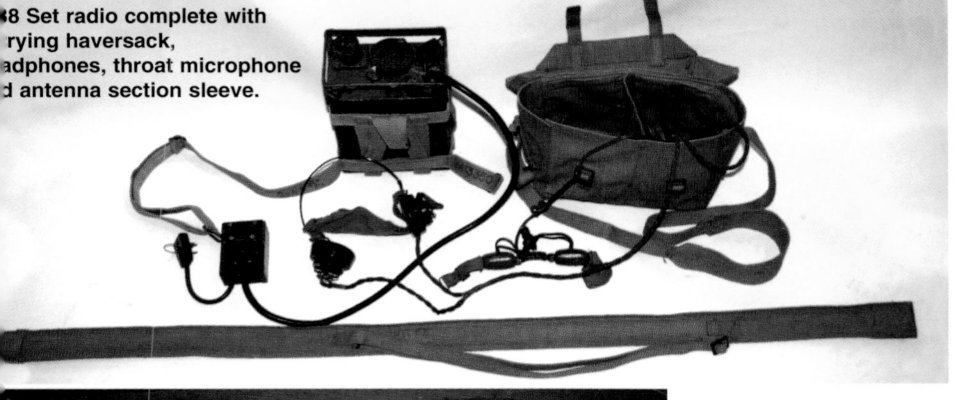

8 Set radio complete with
rying haversack,
adphones, throat microphone
d antenna section sleeve.

The detailed model of LONE HOUSE and HENRY used to plan and rehearse the raid. This model can be seen in the Airborne Forces Museum at Duxford.

The beach at Redcliff Point in Dorset where the evacuation rehearsals took place on 16 February 1942. Weymouth is in the background.

The control tower at Thruxton, which is still in use, with one of the original Nissen huts in the foreground.

SHEET 6.

AIRCRAFT LETTER Y AIRCRAFT NUMBER...... ORDER OF TAKE-OFF 6.

CREW:

Captain. Sjt. CLOW. Observer. Sjt. FRANKLIN.

Observer. Sjt. BRADBURY. W/Operator. Sjt. CLARKE.

Air gunner. Sjt. CHISHOLM.

TROOPS.

Section Name. HARDY. Section Cmdr: Major FROST

1. C.S.M. STRACHAN W. 2. Sjt. FLEMING.

3. TAYLOR 4. SCOTT.

5. Major FROST. 6. McLEOD.

7. L/Cpl. DOBSON. 8. HAYHURST.

9. F/Sgt. COX (R.A.F.) 10. HALLIWELL.

CONTAINERS:

Cell No.	MARKINGS. Bands.	Letters.	Lights.	CONTENTS.
		E.2.	Orange.	TROLLEY.
	2	F.2.	Purple.	EXPLOSIVES ETC. 38 W/T Set.

1545 hours Aircraft leave dispersal sites.

1615 hours Aircraft lined up on perimeter track.

1615 hours Containers delivered to aircraft.

1630 hours Container loading commences.

1730 hours Container loading completed.

1745 hours Aircraft inspected.

2030 hours Paratroops arrive.

2140 hours Paratroopsmarch to aircraft.

2200 hours Emplaning completed.

2215 hours 1st aircraft takes off.

2230 hours Last aircraft takes off.

....
Controller.

One of the twelve original aircraft manifests for the operation. It is for Aircraft Y flown by Sgt Clow and was the 6th to take off. It carried the HARDY section containing Major Frost, CSM Strachan and Flt Sgt Cox.

C Coy, 2nd Bn The Parachute Regiment
Bulford September 1942

Known Bruneval participants are named left to right:

Rear Row: **4th Pte A Young, 7th Pte ED Freeman, 8th Pte RA Conroy, 9th Pte RI Scott, 12th LCpl FOB Murphy, 13th Pte H Flitcroft, 14th Pte PJ O'Neil, 16th Pte F Welch.**
4th Row: **2nd LCpl HC Matkin, 5th Pte C Branwhite, 10th Pte A Ewing, 12th Cpl F Barnett, 14th Pte H McCann, 15th Pte F Creighton, 16th Pte PL Venters, 19th Pte W Addie, 20th Pte A Synyer, 21st Pte JG Crutchley.**
3rd Row: **1st Pte W Beattie, 2nd Pte J Hutchinson, 5th Cpl W Burns, 6th Cpl A Webster, 8th Pte R Draper, 9th Pte J McLeod, 11th Pte JR Coates, 13th Pte T Galey, 14th Pte RT Johnstone, 16th Pte J Hayhurst, 18th Pte F McAusland, 21st Pte P Buchanan, 22nd Pte G Cadden.**

2nd Row: 1st Cpl RW Dobson, 2nd Cpl H Dickie, 4th Sgt G Heslop, 5th Sgt J Judge, 6th Sgt AE Finney, 7th Sgt D Grieve, 8th Sgt J Boyd, 11th Maj JG Ross, 13th CSM GA Strachan, 15th Sgt JL Sharpe, 16th Sgt G Fleming, 17th Sgt W MacFarlane, 18th Sgt T Laughland, 19th Sgt A Gibbons, 20th Sgt V Stewart, 21st CSgt JP Tasker, 22nd LCpl R Stirling.
Front row: 3rd LCpl F Williamson, 5th Pte P McCormack, 11th LCpl SA Hughes, 12th Pte J Calderwood, 16th Pte GW Taylor.

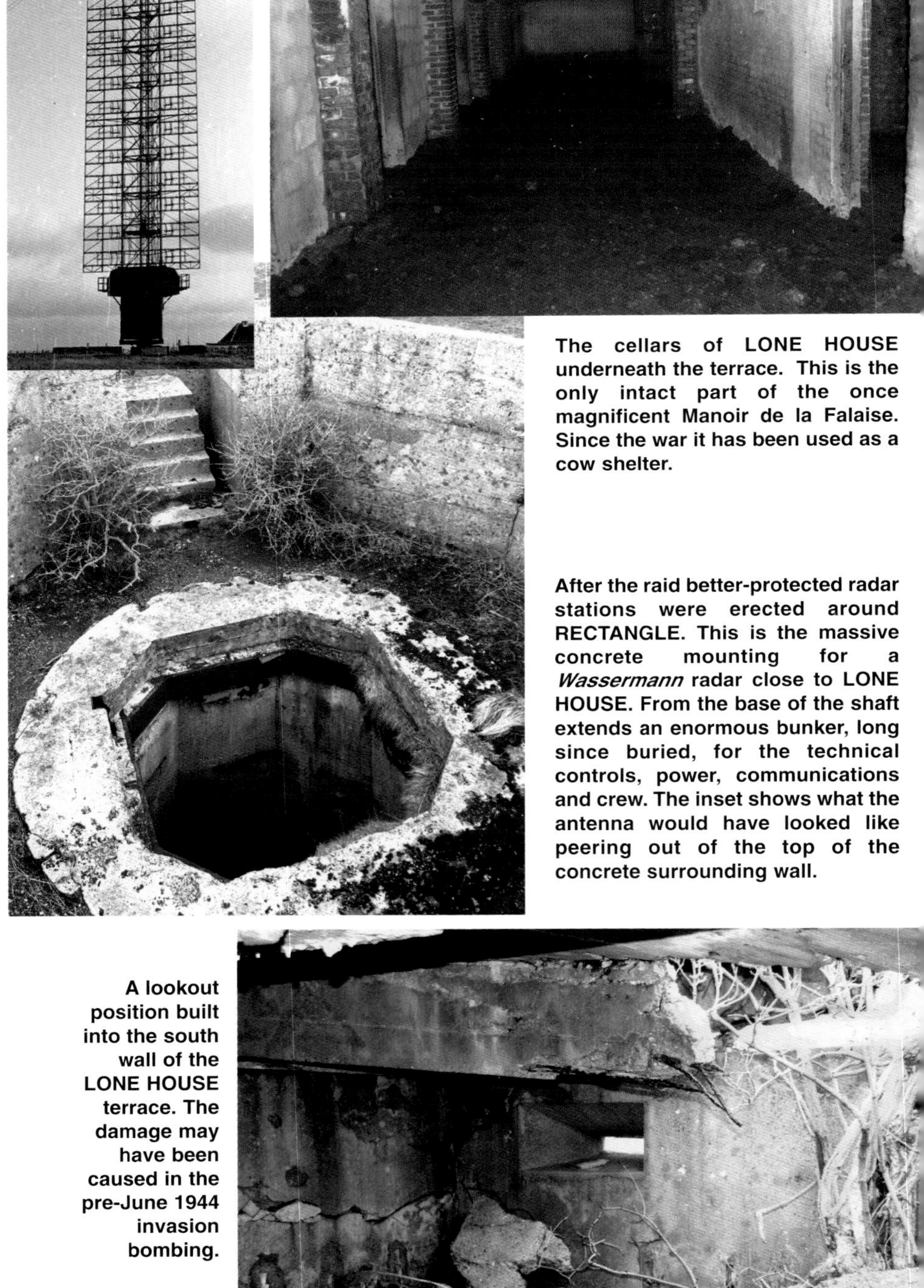

The cellars of LONE HOUSE underneath the terrace. This is the only intact part of the once magnificent Manoir de la Falaise. Since the war it has been used as a cow shelter.

After the raid better-protected radar stations were erected around RECTANGLE. This is the massive concrete mounting for a *Wassermann* radar close to LONE HOUSE. From the base of the shaft extends an enormous bunker, long since buried, for the technical controls, power, communications and crew. The inset shows what the antenna would have looked like peering out of the top of the concrete surrounding wall.

A lookout position built into the south wall of the LONE HOUSE terrace. The damage may have been caused in the pre-June 1944 invasion bombing.

An early 20th Century view of Stella Maris. This building has been replaced with another on a similar ground plan, but it seems never to have been completed.

Above: The slightly raised bank that once surrounded the *Wurzburg*. There is a collapsed dug-out beyond it to the left and RECTANGLE is in the right distance.

Below: The memorial plaque on the barn at Le Tilleul where Privates Embury and Cornell sheltered immediately after the raid. The dedication ceremony in 1994 was attended by George Embury's widow, Ivy, and other members of his family.

ıter pillbox on the southern corner of :TANGLE. The mounting suggests it sed a small anti-tank gun. After the raid whole area around RECTANGLE, uding LONE HOUSE was surrounded by ınti-tank ditch.

house from which the farmer's son saw ɔury and Cornell in the barn (behind ıera) on the morning after the raid.

Above: The current memori
looking south with Point 10
beyond. Additions were mad
in time for the main 70t
anniversary commemoration
in June 2012.

Left: A stone laid as part of th
original Bruneval memorial i
1947.

Right: Mountbatten's summary of the raid, which can be seen on the current memorial at Bruneval. It supports Flt Sgt Cox's post-raid report that the parts of the radar not returned to Britain were destroyed. This is not mentioned by any of the other participants.

Paratroopers exiting a Whitley.

where each man threw off his parachute harness. There was no enemy reaction, but flak from the main *Freya* radar site was being directed at the retreating bombers as they headed home.

Private Scott 335 in RODNEY Aircraft C was hit in the air by a container, lost his fighting knife and the leg of his trousers was ripped open. A few days later back at Tilshead, despite two black eyes and slight concussion, he got no sympathy from Sergeant Forsysth who accused him of making bad exit. While on leave in Richmond, Yorkshire in a pub Scott overheard someone talking about delivering paratroopers to France. Scott said he was one and discovered the other man was Flight Lieutenant Bill Broadley, Pickard's navigator.

Sergeant Cook's aircraft (X), carrying Sergeant Lumb's RODNEY stick, had two problems. The first half of the stick was dropped in the wrong place close to where Charteris and Grieve came down. Then No.6 hung up and had to be dragged back inside. He and the remainder jumped successfully onto the correct DZ the second time around, but about five minutes later and without any equipment as the containers dropped after No.5 on the first attempt.

Having completed the drop each aircraft increased speed and headed out to sea for the return, using the same route as the outward journey. Pickard dived to fifteen metres and left the coast at the lighthouse. The first aircraft landed at Thruxton at 0140 and the last fifty minutes later. Pickard was debriefed and then had a short rest before heading for the Operations Room at Portsmouth to await Frost's return.

Cox was in the same aircraft as Frost and recalled the jumping order differently. Cox says Strachan was the stick commander and last out at No.10, Frost was No.3 and Cox No.6. None of this agrees with the manifest, which has Strachan No.1, Frost No.5 and Cox No.9. However, the manifest seems to have the most sensible jumping order, positioning Frost in the middle of the stick.

As Cox exited the aircraft he heard the command for the man behind to jump. He felt the tug as the parachute opened, saw the Whitley disappearing over his head and the ground coming up towards him. He landed with a gentle bump and, having shrugged himself out of the parachute harness, heard a rustle nearby, which turned out to be one of the two containers on his flight. He joined two sappers searching for the other. As each container was found they disconnected the light to avoid attention. It took ten minutes to unpack, assemble the trolley, load it with the tool bags and other equipment and move off to the RV. Cox could see LONE HOUSE clearly in the moonlight.

The rest were doing very much the same, recovering their weapons and other equipment. Individually they moved to the RV where most relieved themselves of tea and rum. Not very tactical Frost pointed out, but the first act of defiance. Only one man had been injured in the drop, breaking an ankle, but he didn't realise it for another fortnight.

In such clear visibility Frost knew they must have been seen coming down, so speed was of the essence. Everything was going well, so it came as a shock when Ross told him that two sections of NELSON had not turned up and it was unclear if they had been shot down or landed in the wrong place.

Offshore it was very quiet. Cook's orders were to approach the beach cautiously if he had heard nothing from the raiders by 0230. If he found the beach held by the enemy, he was to withdraw to England forthwith. Whatever happened he was to leave by 0315 at the latest in order to be clear of the French coast before first light.

Chapter Eight

THE BATTLE

TWENTY of NELSON's forty men, including its commander Lieutenant Charteris, had been dropped two kms short of the DZ. Charteris made a gentle landing, but there was so little wind the parachute fell around him. Having extricated himself he moved off southwest as planned to meet up with his batman in the other stick commanded by Sergeant Grieve, while the rest recovered their equipment from the containers and made their way to meet him. He realized immediately he was in the wrong place; a nasty moment and he felt lost. He watched other aircraft flying straight and level as though they had yet to drop their sticks and deduced correctly they had been dropped short. He met his men, told them the problem and how if they went north they could still reach their objective.

The position where Charteris' and Grieve's NELSON sticks landed. On the skyline extreme right is the real DZ. Left of it is RECTANGLE and left again is the faint outline of the foundations of LONE HOUSE. Below the centre of RECTANGLE is a small clump of bushes, the RV. Charteris and Grieve set off to the left initially.

Part of another stick landed close to Charteris. This turned out to be the first half of Sergeant Lumb's stick from X aircraft. Charteris told Lumb where they were, to get his stick together and follow on behind heading due north. He then set off with his section in diamond formation followed by Sergeant Grieve's section.

Charteris knew he was short of time if he was to secure the

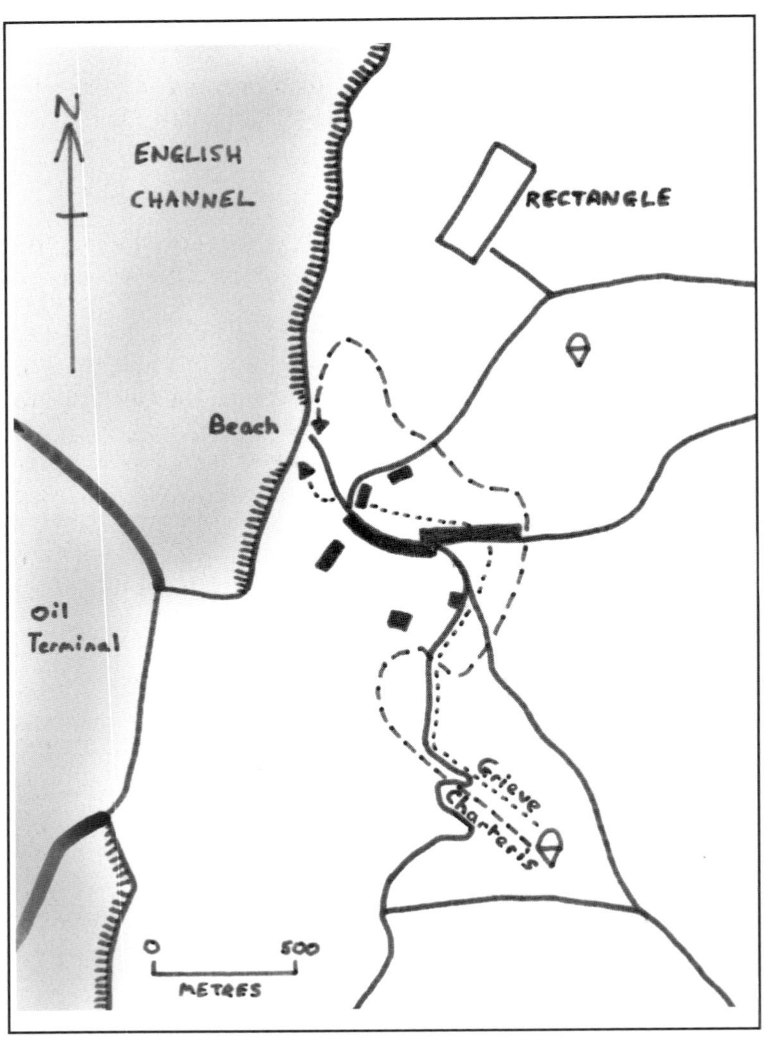

The separate routes taken by Charteris and Grieve. Previous accounts have shown one or the other route and either attribute Grieve's route to Charteris or show both sections using the same route. One even shows Charteris attacking down the length of the east-west road in the ravine, something that neither section attempted.

beach before the main force began the withdrawal. He set off at a fast lope of about ten kilometres per hour and after covering 1,200 metres saw the lighthouse and soon after the wood at RECTANGLE. The loom of the lighthouse confirmed they were going in the right direction.

They crossed the north-south road leading to Bruneval. Across a field Charteris saw the dark edge of a wood just as they came under fire. Private Sutherland was hit in the shoulder and was unable to keep up; he was subsequently captured. The rest dodged into the wood. A Bren covered them while they turned at right angles and moved through the wood with the intention of turning left and rushing up its other side to come between the village and the beach.

Charteris was about to move off again when he heard a screech. Turning he saw a German five metres away and raised his Colt, but failed to release the safety catch. The German fired once ineffectively and was then hit by a full Sten magazine from Sergeant Gibbons. The German had walked alongside one of his men for a while thinking they were also Germans, before discovering his mistake.

Having encountered the enemy south of Bruneval, Charteris had to modify his plan and go inland to pass east of the village. They went through some scrubby difficult country to reach the edge of Bruneval, which they plunged into making lots of noise, but Charteris judged speed was more important than silence. At the bottom of the valley they reached a road with open ground on either side. He positioned a Bren to cover them while they doubled over. Climbing the other side of the valley they were fired upon again and due to the vegetation on the hillside Charteris' section became separated. The rear half of the section turned left into the wood and Charteris lost touch with them.

Charteris could hear a Bren firing and deduced the rest of the attack was going ahead according to plan. Corporal Hill was sent back to find the missing half section, but failed to make contact and returned to Charteris. The four lost men under Private Matkin moved independently and reached the beach after it was captured. On the way they went round the edge of the village and avoided a crowd of Germans.

In the other section, Sergeant Grieve quickly got his men to sort out their gear on the DZ while two scouts found the road leading to Bruneval. The two sappers were too overloaded to carry all their equipment and abandoned the mines in favour of the Polish mine detector. The Royal Engineer post-raid report admitted the amount of equipment the sappers took was just about impossible to carry in action.

Grieve's section became separated from Charteris soon after

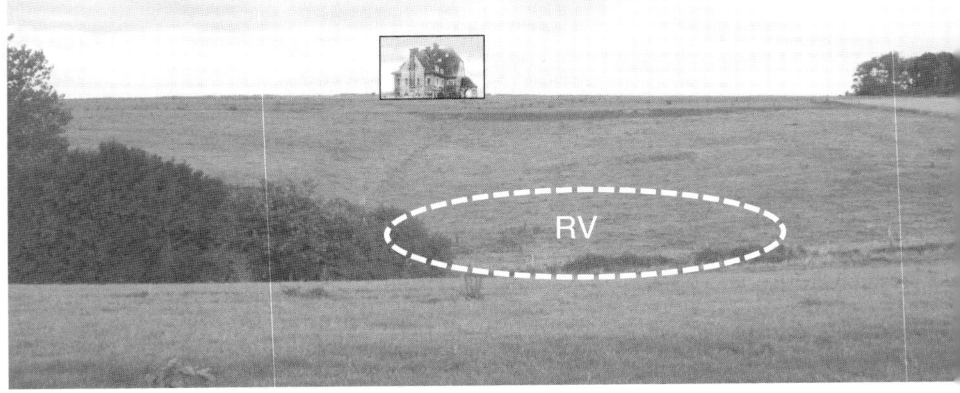

From the western edge of the DZ - the RV is in the re-entrant by the trees. RECTANGLE is on the right and LONE HOUSE stood just left of centre on the skyline. Below is the low bank where Cox and the sappers awaited the call forward to HENRY. (Demolished house added for orientation)

leaving the DZ. To make up time Grieve decided there was no option other than to use the road and they set off towards the beach at a trot. He then moved his section through the woods south of Bruneval during which they dispatched a German with a knife and a few others later in weapon slits.

Meanwhile, having landed on the proper DZ, the other twenty NELSON men arrived at the RV, one light section and the heavy section. The light section was the one under Sergeant Tasker, detailed to clear REDOUBT on the cliff north of the beach on the evacuation route. It set off, found the position unmanned and took control of it.

Frost had to get on with the priorities of HENRY and LONE HOUSE. As he left the RV he told Ross to wait a few minutes to see if Charteris turned up. If not, he was to take the heavy section and do what he could to seize the beach. When the radar

The RV was in the foreground with the DZ off to the left. Sergeant Tasker's light section headed off along the high ground on the right to seize REDOUBT. Captain Ross took the heavy section down the re-entrant in the centre towards the beach.

Manior de la Falaise (LONE HOUSE) before the war. The entrance way through which Frost entered the house is on the right. Other members of the assault party entered simultaneously from the terrace into the first floor on the left.

had been secured Frost would send DRAKE to help him, but couldn't release DRAKE or RODNEY until their primary roles had been achieved.

JELLICOE, HARDY and DRAKE took only ten minutes to gather at the RV. Having shaken out into battle formations they moved off swiftly. They met no opposition, but a few rounds were heard and it seemed that some enemy were alert. DRAKE headed off to take up its position silently between LONE HOUSE and RECTANGLE. RODNEY took up position in rear of the assault parties and waited.

Frost's men, including Newman, surrounded LONE HOUSE silently. JELLICOE made directly for HENRY keeping to the left of LONE HOUSE. A short distance behind Vernon, Cox and the sapper detachment hauled the three trolleys over a succession of barbed wire obstacles. They went so far then sheltered behind a low bank awaiting the call forward. While waiting Cox heard a Mills grenade explode and firing coming from the village.

Frost was surprised to discover the front door of LONE HOUSE wide open. In training he had encouraged everyone to add ideas and ask questions. One man asked what to do if the door was locked, another suggested helpfully he ring the bell.

Bob Hilton (left) and Andrew Duff during the filming of the complimentary Pen & Sword dvd at the entrance to the demolished LONE HOUSE. They are standing on the original entrance floor tiles.

When JELLICOE had encircled HENRY, Frost blew his whistle. He recalled, 'Immediately explosions, yells and the sound of automatic fire came from the proximity of the radar set.'

Frost led the charge into the chateau with six men, who threw in grenades and sprayed the downstairs rooms with Sten guns. At the same time others burst in through the windows on the opposite side of the house. The ground floor was empty. They heard shooting above them and rushed upstairs shouting 'Surrender', 'Hande Hoch'and some obscenities. In one room a German was firing through a window at JELLICOE; he was killed immediately by a burst of Sten gun fire. The rest of the chateau was devoid of people and even furniture. A prisoner later confirmed it had been abandoned since September 1941 after an incendiary bomb had crashed through the roof and landed on the bed of a *Feldwebel*. Thereafter they slept in a dugout left by a flak unit that had previously occupied the *Würzburg* site.

Hearing Frost's signal Lieutenant Young, Sergeant McKenzie and three others in the JELLICOE team rushed into the radar site with grenades and Sten guns. Surprise was complete. A sentry challenged them and then opened fire before being cut down.

They rapidly cleared the dugouts and trenches, killing most of the garrison, but some fled. The German post-action report states a grenade killed one man, as he was about to detonate a demolition charge to destroy the installation. Young was conscious they did not have a prisoner and saw a German, silhouetted in the moonlight, heading for the cliffs. They gave chase and he fell over the edge, but managed to cling onto a ledge three metres below. Young burst out laughing as the German tried to climb back up the cliff with his hands in the air. He was hauled up, found to be unarmed and was taken back to the radar.

The prisoner's version of events is similar. He had been asleep in the dugout until 0100 when he was woken in haste with a warning that British aircraft were overhead. The off-duty operators ran towards the radar installation, but then realised that paratroopers had entered the site from the south. Two made a hurried escape northwards. The *Unteroffizier* dashed to the lookout post and returned with the French light machine gun. He fired a short burst before being cut down. The paratroopers then cleared the shelters and killed anyone who had not fled. The prisoner said he made his way around the tool dugout to the cliff edge where he attempted to conceal himself, but fell about five metres until grasping a projecting rock. When he climbed back up he was taken prisoner by an officer. He saw the paratroopers throwing grenades at the radar cabin and was impressed with their speed of action, but less so when they bunched crossing barbed wire and on the beach later. Coincidentally, Lieutenant Charteris also commented on unprofessional behaviour later at the beach.

Arriving at the radar, Vernon found Young who briefed him on what had happened so far. The dugouts up to the cliff had been cleared and Young had shot a German coming out of one of them. He said he had also been into the chateau and there was nothing of interest there. However, it seems unlikely Young would have had time to visit the chateau in the few minutes that elapsed since the attack commenced.

Vernon conducted a quick inspection of the installation before either sending a sapper to collect the rest of the party or shouting, 'Come on the REs'. The party reached the radar eight minutes later. The installation consisted of the apparatus and three dugouts, one for tools, another with electric lighting for the off shift night duty crew to sleep in and a third for the power distribution.

As soon as he knew it was secure, Frost left twelve men to hold LONE HOUSE and ran with his batman to the radar. He found Young who was being remonstrated with by Sergeant McKenzie, who called him a 'cruel bastard'. There was some justification for this accusation as their orders were to bring back radar operators as prisoners and JELLICOE appeared to have succeeded in killing five out of six of them. In reality they had not killed anything like that number, but the fact remained, they only had one prisoner.

Frost made rapid dispositions to defend the site as by then fire was being received from RECTANGLE. Rifleman McIntyre was killed near the front door of LONE HOUSE when Frost brought the party out to cover the radar site. Frost then joined Newman with the radar operator prisoner, who wore a blue *Luftwaffe* uniform. Newman questioned the badly shaken man:

> *Even if he was a bloody cleaner, he must know something. I tore the swastika badge from his uniform for my personal satisfaction. Then I started to interrogate him about the number of German troops and their positions – we only had some information till then – and I thought he was lying. So I shook him by his lapels and said so, and my comrade said we should kill him. But I said no as we had to have prisoners and he was very young and started to cry and was shaking with fear, so I said we should take him along.*

The prisoner said there were 1,000 troops in the immediate area, but having received a hefty belt on the jaw from Sergeant McKenzie, confirmed the troops around RECTANGLE numbered no more than 100, but they were well armed. They had mortars, but as they were mainly *Luftwaffe* personnel,were not familiar with them. The majority of the garrison was stationed further inland.

The prisoner was so glad to be spared, he gave Sergeant McKenzie his watch, who took it on leave, had it cleaned and a new glass fitted. On return to the unit he was told the prisoner had complained about the theft of his watch and McKenzie was obliged to return it. Having forked out 5/- for repairs, he was not amused.

Cox noticed the paratroopers had taken up kneeling positions around the radar as he met Vernon. He got over the barbed wire fence (three metres thick but only 0.6 metres high), set back forty-five metres in a circle around the radar. Cox believed it was low to avoid interfering with the set. Having struggled over a number of wire fences with the trolley by then, he believed rucksacks would have been more useful.

An attempt was made by Vernon to photograph the radar dish with a Leica camera. He quickly discovered that the flash brought a great deal of unwanted attention from two machine guns at RECTANGLE. Fortunately most German fire was directed at LONE HOUSE and DRAKE rather than the dismantling party around the radar, but some rounds hit the dish. Firing could also be heard coming from RODNEY. Frost suggested to Vernon he might care to stop using the flash. The picture he took was in any case double exposed. Although some

Below: The double exposed photograph taken by Lieutenant Vernon of the *Würzburg* radar dish at Bruneval. Details of claimed victories painted on the inside of the dish can be made out, but little else except the three huts at Tilshead.

Above: These are believed to be the same huts shown in Vernon's photograph in 2010. The low earth blast protection walls and telegraph poles have been removed and the huts in the centre distance in Vernon's picture appear to have been demolished, but otherwise little has changed.

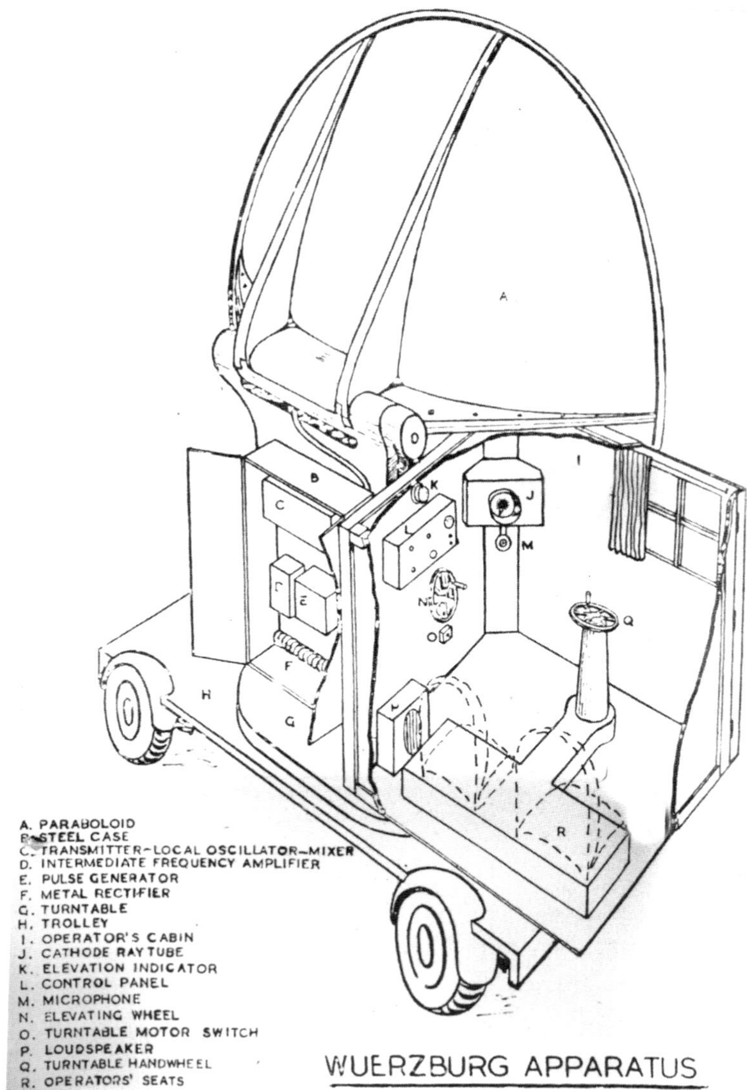

A diagram of the *Würzburg* station compiled from notes and sketches made by the dismantling party andfrom interrogating the *Luftwaffe* prisoner.

details of the radar dish are visible, most of the picture is of three huts at Tilshead.

Cox traced the antenna lead back to the equipment compartment on the rear of the dish; it was 0.9 metres wide, 0.6 metres deep and 1.5 metres high. He tore aside the thick black rubber curtain shielding the equipment and called, 'Hey Peter

Don Preist with the sawn off antenna element.

(Newman), this thing's still hot. Ask the Jerry if he was tracking our aircraft as we came in.' The German confirmed the *Freya* had picked them up well offshore and alerted the *Würzburg*, which picked them up about thirty kilometres out, but they had turned it off when they realised the aircraft were heading straight for them.

Cox and the sappers continued examining the radar, making notes and sketches while bullets flew around them. There was some reflected moonlight from the snow to see by and they had hooded torches as well. Cox noted a rotatable platform mounted on a four-wheeled truck with the wheels raised. The radar was surrounded by a 0.6 metres high turf wall topped with duckboards. The whole apparatus was well sandbagged up to platform level. The dish was parabolic, about three metres across and hinged so it could be swung manually up, down or sideways. A small cabin to the side (1.2 x 0.9 x 0.6 metres) sheltered the display screen and operator's seat. The design was clean and straightforward, solid and in good order.

In the equipment compartment they saw the transmitter and the first stage of the receiving equipment at the top. Below were the pulse unit and the rest of the receiver, with the power pack at the bottom. While Cox made notes a sapper smashed off any metal labels he could see with a hammer and chisel.

Vernon set the sappers to work. As there was no quick way of removing the antenna element he ordered one man to simply hacksaw it off. Cox and Corporal Jones removed the pulse unit and receiver, but the transmitter retaining screws could not be reached, even with a very long screwdriver. Cox and Vernon grasped it while a sapper crow-barred it off its mounting; it came away bringing the frame with it. Although they didn't see it at the time the frame contained the antenna switching unit that allowed the dish to be used by transmitter and receiver and was a vital part of the design. They continued crow-barring off the rest of the components, but frequently had to use torches, which attracted ever more accurate fire from RECTANGLE and protests from the paratroopers.

Lieutenant John Timothy was a Marks & Spencer assistant store manager when war broke out. He enlisted in the Grenadier Guards and was commissioned in the Queen's Own Royal West Kent Regiment in December 1940.

The dish proved too big to dismantle and time precluded retrieving the cathode display equipment from the operator's cabin, which was not even entered as the vital equipment was in the external compartment. In any case one of the components taken away did have a small display screen for calibration purposes. Trolleys were loaded with the equipment as enemy fire increased. While the sappers were dismantling the installation, Vernon checked out one of the dugouts in which there was a dead German and a steel box, but it did not contain anything of interest.

The Germans had been quick to react, having tracked the Whitleys and seen the paratroopers leaving the aircraft. All units were alerted and scouts were sent out from the *Freya* station to see what was going on. Troops at RECTANGLE correctly reported that the paratroopers were moving towards the chateau and *Würzburg* and had split into various groups.

The German unit, *I. Companie 685. Infantrie Regiment*, based in La Poterie, was responsible for the coastal defences in the area. Its reserve platoon had just finished an exercise and it was sent west towards the chateau. The *Feldwebel* commanding the

Bruneval platoon was already alert when the company commander ordered him to occupy Point 102 to the southeast and the defences near the beach. The *Feldwebel* divided his force into two groups for the move to the battle positions and it was these troops that were encountered by Charteris and Grieve.

At the beach the German NCO in charge was already alert and went outside when he heard the approaching aircraft. A few minutes later he was called back inside to take a phone call from Company HQ. Having been told what was going on he brought his section together. Looking outside again he saw movement on the north cliffs and fired a white flare, then his machine pistol high in the air towards them. Convinced they were enemy he decided to move the light machine gun from the beach to behind the house and prepared to bar the way to the beach to anyone coming from the high ground to the north. Grenades were issued and the whole section occupied the disjointed trenches behind the house within eight minutes of the first alarm. One man (Schmidt) was left behind to man the telephone and two others to guard the beach.

Frost could hear firing all around. From the direction of the beach a machine gun was answered by a Bren and white flares were periodically going up. Three vehicles on sidelights had arrived at RECTANGLE carrying the reserve platoon from La Poterie and fire from there was increasing in volume and spreading as the German reinforcements deployed. DRAKE was returning the fire and Frost expected a counter-attack towards HENRY and LONE HOUSE. RODNEY was also fully engaged with RECTANGLE. As his 38 Set was not working, Lieutenant Timothy sent a runner to assure Frost they were under control. Firing could also be heard from the direction of the village; unknown to Frost this was Charteris' and Grieve's sections

Now overgrown, this is the area of dead ground where the dismantling party took cover after CSM Strachan and another man had been wounded by machine-gun fire. RECTANGLE is in the distance.

attempting to get to the beach.

Frost claimed he was bedeviled by poor communications and had to resort to runners and whistle signals. However, the post-raid report says the 38 Sets worked well with one exception in which the throat mike fell apart; perhaps this was RODNEY's radio. In addition, the rigid organisation forced on Frost by the plan denied him a functioning Company HQ. He sent a runner to Lieutenant Nauomoff for DRAKE to fall back through the main party and lead the way to the beach. He reminded the runner to identify himself with the password, as appearing suddenly behind men in action could be dangerous.

Frost did not know if NELSON had cleared the evacuation beach, but with pressure increasing on every side and the noise of vehicles to the east, he decided it was time to settle for whatever the sappers had and head for the beach. The longer they waited the greater the chance the Germans would bring mortars to bear. The action at the objective had taken just over fifteen minutes.

As DRAKE withdrew from its blocking position they threw grenades and opened heavy fire on the enemy at RECTANGLE to discourage them from following too closely. The others then followed for the beach. The dismantling party discovered it was easier to carry the radar components on their shoulders and abandoned the trolleys. Cox recalled an explosion and turning, saw the site of the radar had gone up; he is the only eyewitness to mention this. However, a bronze plaque on the memorial quoting Mountbatten records the paratroopers, '.... removed vital components of the new German radar station and completely destroyed the rest of it'.

When DRAKE caught up with the main party, Frost told Nauomoff he was likely to have to fight for the beach and to try to contact Ross who was 'somewhere down there'. Nauomoff set off and got down undetected, but as the main party crested the skyline a voice below shouted that the boats had arrived and they should come down. Almost simultaneously they came under machine-gun fire from the GUARD ROOM pillbox on the opposite hillside. CSM Strachan and another man were wounded beside REDOUBT, which had earlier been occupied by one of NELSON's light sections. Frost got Strachan into some dead ground, dressed three abdominal wounds (he had seven in total) and gave him morphine. Cox saw the grass around his feet

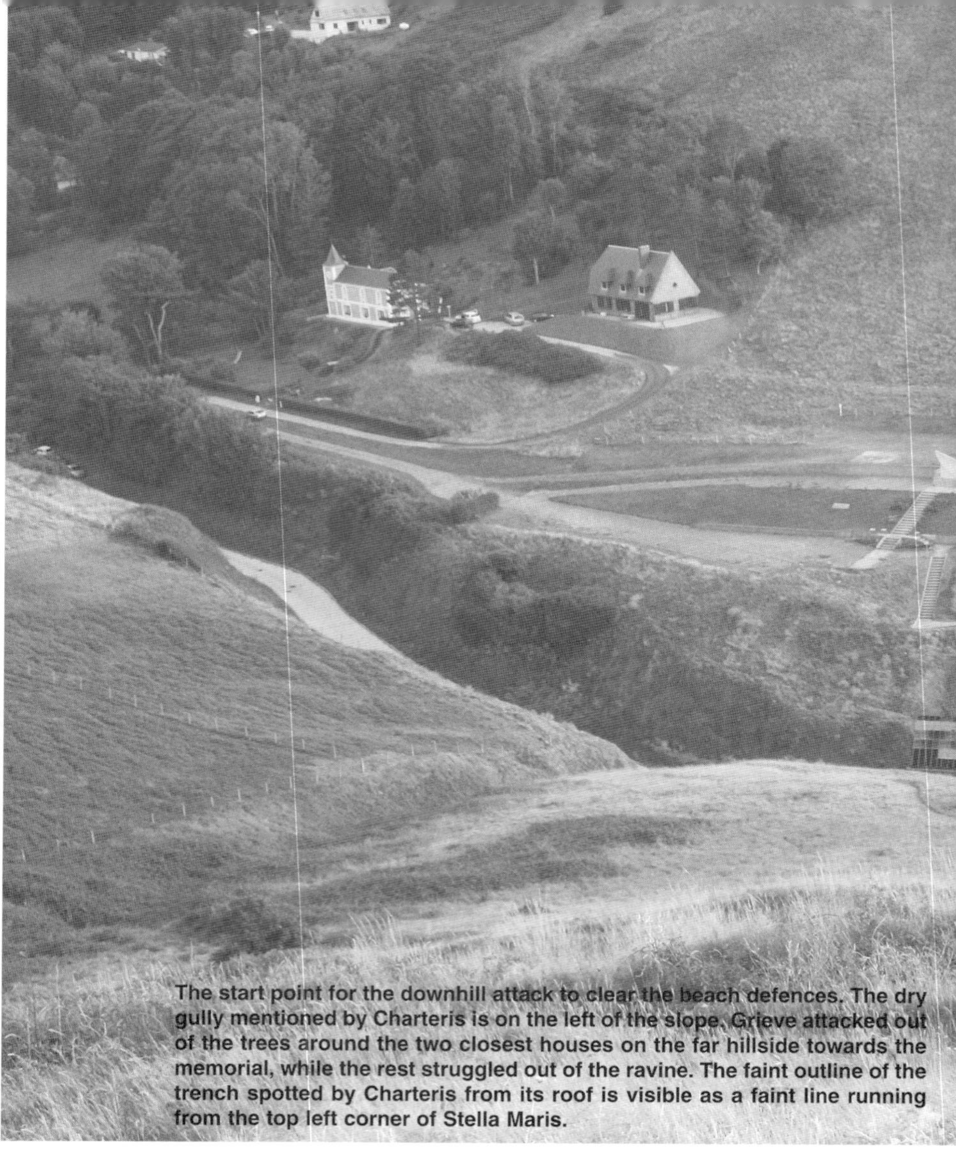

The start point for the downhill attack to clear the beach defences. The dry gully mentioned by Charteris is on the left of the slope. Grieve attacked out of the trees around the two closest houses on the far hillside towards the memorial, while the rest struggled out of the ravine. The faint outline of the trench spotted by Charteris from its roof is visible as a faint line running from the top left corner of Stella Maris.

disturbed by passing bullets before he took cover and the piece of equipment in his hand was hit, but not seriously damaged.

Ross shouted up not to come down as the beach was not yet secure. Frost realised the two other NELSON sticks must still be missing and had been unable to achieve their objective. He sent Young with a mixed section of ten men from DRAKE, HARDY and JELLICOE down to help Ross seize the beach defences and

then went to the cliff edge to flash the letter F seaward with his torch; but did not receive an answer.

A runner appeared from RODNEY saying the Germans were advancing from RECTANGLE and had reoccupied LONE HOUSE. It was vital to keep the Germans away while the beach was secured. Frost told the dismantling party to remain in cover until the machine gun had been silenced, while he took every

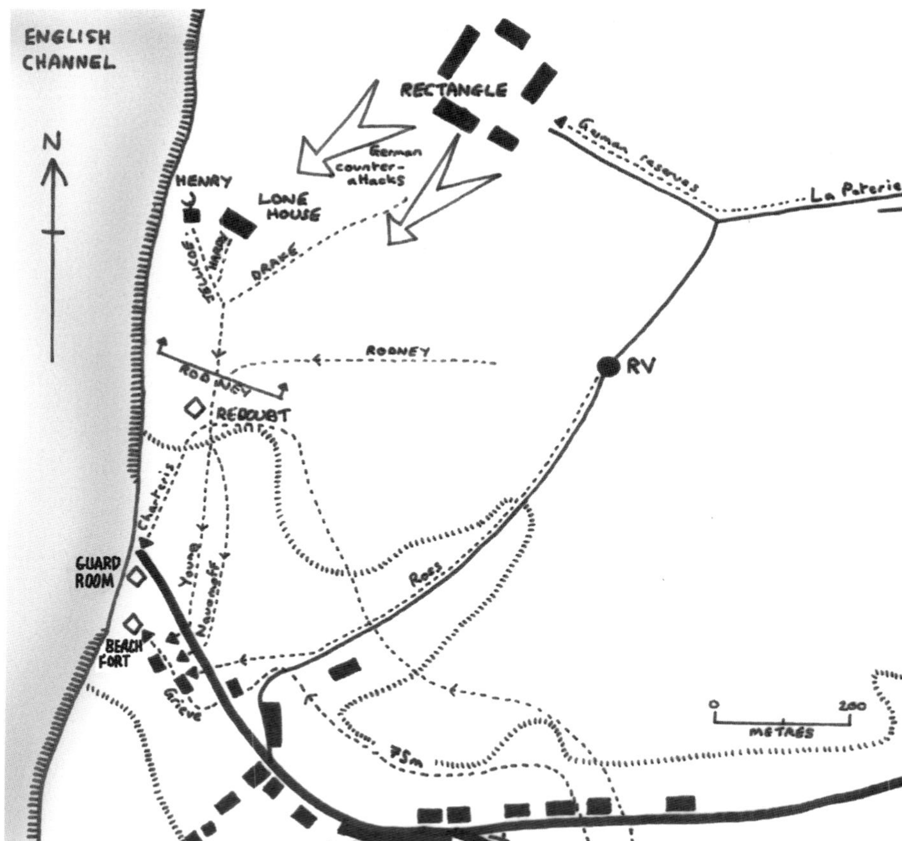

Withdrawal to the evacuation beach. Frost pulled DRAKE, HARDY and JELLICOE back to REDOUBT, while RODNEY covered the rear against German counter-attacks from RECTANGLE. Frost sent Nauomoff's section to contact Ross and soon after sent an ad hoc section under Young to join them. Meanwhile Grieve manoeuvred into position south of GUARD ROOM and it was his determined rush, supported by elements of Ross', Naoumoff's and Young's sections that overcame the beach defences. Simultaneously Charteris' half section seized Stella Maris.

available man, including Vernon, to counter-attack with RODNEY. However, the enemy seemed confused and did not follow up, so Frost cancelled the counter-attack, left Timothy to hold the hilltop and hurried back to control the fight for the beach.

The Germans were indeed confused. The mis-dropped sticks

led to the Bruneval platoon being sent to other tasks rather than advancing on HENRY and LONE HOUSE. Had it done so the results of the raid may have been very different.

Meanwhile Sergeant Grieve had worked his way north of the east-west road. He then led his section back over it and turned sharp right towards the German defences on the south side and the sea. They paused for a few moments to catch their breath, relieved to have made it.

Ross had waited at the RV with the NELSON heavy section, while Frost deployed the rest of the force. Ross then led the section down to the beach road. The original plan envisaged the three light sections attacking the beach strong points simultaneously with Ross' heavy section in reserve providing fire support, but he had only two sections to achieve this. The one light section that had arrived at the RV under Sergeant Tasker had silently occupied REDOUBT on the cliff to the north of the beach where Strachan was wounded. With that side of the ravine under control, Ross intended securing the other side around GUARD ROOM with the heavy section before both sections cleared down to the beach.

Ross had his batman, Sergeant Sharp, two signalers to contact the Navy, two sappers, two Bren gunners and a runner. As the heavy section emerged from the trees the movement was seen and a white flare rose from GUARD ROOM. The section was soon pinned down by machine-gun fire from slit trenches on the landward side of GUARD ROOM, where there also appeared to be six or seven rifles firing. This was the German section deployed earlier from BEACH FORT. Ross replied, but the position of the trenches meant they were not visible to Sergeant Tasker's light section above. Sharp crawled to the barbed wire across the road and tried to cut a way through. Ross later said he would have given a lot for some mortars just then.

As he shouted out his warning to the main force on the cliffs above, Ross realized that the Germans pinning his section down had been distracted. They found a knife rest gate in the perimeter wire and pulled it aside to make an opening, just as Nauomoff's section reached the bottom of the slope. The combined force was just about to rush through the wire and assault the German position when they heard the war cry of the Seaforth Highlanders, 'Caber Feigh' (the deer's antlers). They assumed this came from Charteris' two sections, but it was actually only Grieve's section that hurled themselves at the defences from the southeast. Ross' section reverted to its original role and laid down covering fire.

Charteris' section, by then only four strong, had pressed on at speed keeping the firing from the beach on their left side. Charteris found Timothy who told him the Germans held the beach and one NELSON section was pinned down at the bottom of the valley. HARDY and JELLICOE were in position in a dip on the edge of the valley. Charteris found Frost, who was most surprised to see him. Frost was concerned because he didn't really know what was happening in the valley. The troops he had were mainly armed with Stens, which did not have the range to engage the Germans holding them up below.

Frost decided to attack down the hill and ordered Charteris to do so. Charteris only had three men with him (Sergeant Gibbons and Corporals Laughland and Hill). They were exhausted having carried much more than Charteris, so he took Hill's rifle and give him his Colt. Hill was carrying four Bren pan magazines, which came in handy later when another section's Bren ran out of ammunition.

Charteris says the various parties were all mixed up and they set off together. He found himself going down a dry gully and felt naked only sixty-five metres from BEACH FORT. They lay down at the wire above the sunken road and threw two volleys of grenades onto the house balcony, then charged over the road and entered the house after tossing more grenades into the cellar. Charteris had trouble finding the front door, because it was at the back.

Once inside the house Charteris opened a door and encountered a German with his hands up, who was relieved of his grenades. This was the telephonist, Schmidt, who had been trying to explain on the phone to an irate *Major* that the noise disturbing him was the sound of enemy grenades going off inside the house. Schmidt could not safely leave the building so turned off the light and hid in an inner room. The British burst in spraying their Stens around. He could see them, but not *vice versa*, and wondered if he should open fire, but couldn't bring himself to do so and sensibly decided to surrender. He said he was taken prisoner by Sergeant Sharp.

From the roof Charteris spotted a trench cut into the hillside leading from the yard at the back of the house. Back downstairs

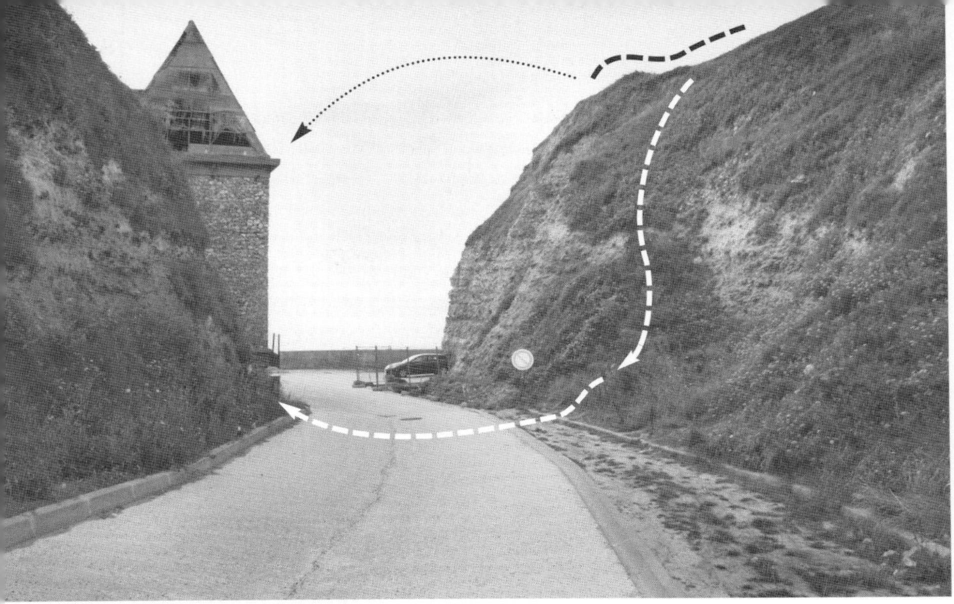

Charteris' half section reached the edge of the ravine on the right to shower Stella Maris on the left with grenades, before descending to the road to storm the building.

he threw a grenade into the trench, but it got caught in netting and didn't go off. Ross arrived and gave Charteris more grenades, about the same time as Sergeant Mackenzie joined him.

Charteris was about to bomb another dugout when a wounded German soldier inside (Tewes) surrendered to Lieutenant Young. In his interrogation he stated he had taken the light machine gun from its position behind the house so it could be set up in the pillbox and had then been sent back to BEACH FORT to get flare pistol ammunition. The fire from the attackers had grown in intensity and he was sent back for more grenades. He came under heavy fire and was hit, so took cover in the other pillbox.

Meanwhile the pillbox above BEACH FORT had been attacked with grenades. One German was killed, another wounded and the sergeant, realising he was being engaged from two sides, decided to withdraw the survivors southwards into the woods. Charteris sited a Bren to cover towards the wood in case they returned.

Corporal Campbell, from the RODNEY half section that landed close to Charteris, was sent by Sergeant Lumb to find out what was happening. Charteris told him to bring forward the rest with the radio, as Ross needed it on the beach. Charteris then posted his men about fifty metres inland in the German defences to cover the rear of the beach. Back in the road Charteris saw CSM Strachan, by then talking nonsense due to the morphine. Charteris searched a prisoner (presumably Tewes or Schmidt), while a gaggle of paratroopers stood around snarling, but caused him no harm. Charteris made an interesting comment in his report, that they were not very well trained and did not really know what to do. Shortly after, Charteris met up with Sergeant Grieve for the first time since leaving the DZ.

During the assault Corporal Stewart in Grieve's section was struck by a splinter in the head. He called out to his mate, Private Freeman, he'd had it and gave him his wallet. Freeman checked the wound and told him it was only, 'a wee bit of a gash', at which Stewart leapt up and retorted, 'Gie us ma bluidy wallet back then!'

The sappers quickly confirmed there were no mines on the beach. The sappers with RODNEY laid mines on the road to compensate for those abandoned by NELSON's sappers, but apparently put them in the wrong place.

The dismantling party had waited while the beach defences were cleared. When called they began the climb down, slipping down the cliff path with their heavy booty. Sapper Jackie Mitchell slid the largest radar pieces to the beach, 'riding' them down the cliff to get there faster. Strachan was with them, half walking and being half carried. Under the influence of morphine he was shouting out unintelligible orders. The post-raid medical report commented that the carriage of morphine was good for morale, but it seems to have been used rather lavishly.

A sentry challenged Cox at the bottom of the slope and he gave the password. In the ravine he noticed a German with his hands up and Charteris rushing round shouting for any Germans left to surrender. They moved to the beach where a sapper was sweeping with a mine detector and soon declared it safe. Having got the radar components to the beach and stacked them in a safe place under the cliffs, there was nothing for Cox and the five sappers to do but sit down and wait.

Chapter Nine

EXTRACTION BY SEA AND RETURN

WITH THE BEACH cleared, RODNEY was called in by radio, which is interesting as there were problems with RODNEY's radio earlier. The whole force was assembled on the beach with the equipment, prisoners and wounded at about 0215, but the signalers reported they could not contact the Navy. The 18 Sets had not arrived, one being with the half section of RODNEY that dropped short; it is not clear why the other 18 Set did not arrive. A 38 Set was tried instead. A beacon was also set up to make contact with the companion set in the landing craft.

CSM Strachan was beginning to feel the cold and Lieutenant Timothy lent him a cricket sweater he brought with him to keep warm on the flight. Timothy was later pleased to note that Strachan recovered, but he never got his sweater back.

A pre-war view of the beach at low water before Stella Maris was built. There are very few obstacles.

A modern comparison shows numerous boulders, probably positioned to reduce erosion.

The tide was beginning to fall, bringing back memories of the failed evacuation on Southampton Water. As Timothy's group arrived, almost tumbling down the cliffs, they reported having seen vehicle headlights approaching Bruneval from the east and southeast, indicating more German reinforcements and the prospect of a strong counter-attack. German fire increased from the cliffs and Private Scott 681 was killed. Frost ordered NELSON to guard the inland approaches.

The beach was relatively safe for the moment until the Germans brought heavier weapons such as mortars to bear. A few tense minutes were spent trying to raise the boats by signal lamp. Ross suggested they use the pre-arranged Very pistol signals. Frost agreed and simultaneously green flares were fired to the north and south of the beach. There was no reaction so a second attempt was made with the SOS signals of red Very flares. A light mist was developing and visibility had reduced to no more than 800 metres.

Feeling dispirited Frost went back to arrange the defences to meet the anticipated German counterattack. A fishing boat was spotted. In extremis they worked out they could get the radar components and eight men aboard, in a last ditch attempt to get the equipment back to England. Just as Frost began to believe the raid was about to fail, one of the signalers shouted, 'Sir, the boats are coming in! The boats are here! God bless the ruddy Navy, sir!'

Offshore, Cook had tried contacting the beach at 0145, but received no answer. When the parachute force began assembling, the Navy received the homing signals and could see men on the beach, but with so many flashes, explosions and tracers it was difficult to interpret the 'come-in' signal. Having established they were required, the first two ALCs began their approach at nine knots. They slowed for the final approach using boat hooks to make soundings.

When they were just under 300 metres out, a message was received from the jubilant beach signalers indicating that all boats should come in together. This was a misunderstanding by the signalers rather than a conscious command decision onshore. Nevertheless Cook complied as he could see there was sufficient room for all the landing craft. The six ALCs took seven minutes to reach the beach, arriving at 0235, while the two LCSs guarded the flanks. They were greeted with a cheer from the

ALC *134* during training on Loch Fyne.

paratroopers. The ALCs did not snag any underwater obstacles, but had a few problems with boulders.

The embarked soldiers on the landing craft opened fire where they assumed the Germans were gathering on top of the cliffs. They were not using tracer and to Frost it seemed their fire was directed where his men were positioned to defend the beach. The noise was deafening. Frost and Ross ran to the water's edge shouting and waving for the fire to stop. One of the Bren gunners said to Frost, 'We thought you was a Jerry with a suicide wish, but we gave you the benefit of the doubt.' The fire slowed,

ALC *125* during training on Loch Fyne with the parachute landing Force.

but it turned out the Brens had been firing at the tops of the cliffs anyway. In the circumstances it was clearly impossible for Preist to land to examine the installation.

The deviation from the original evacuation plan and increasing enemy fire caused considerable confusion. However, despite the swell and falling tide the men waded into the water to hold the landing craft stern on to the sea while loading commenced.

The evacuation began with the dismantling party and their precious cargo onto ALC *134* with Preist on board. Cox carried the antenna element and waded out thigh deep to get aboard. The ALC was under fire and soon hard aground on a rock due to being overloaded. Lieutenant Donald Quick, the skipper, ordered half the men into the water to shove the craft off the rock and then managed to get away, but was still badly overloaded. The engines broke down after a few hundred metres and the ALC had to be taken in tow by a MGB. Quick kept the craft afloat through pumping and bailing and both LCSs closed in and took off passengers to lighten the load.

As ALC *125* was beaching, its ketch line ran off the drum and the craft was in danger of broaching. Without waiting for instructions the Coxswain, Able Seaman J T Bland, reversed the engines and kept the craft in deep water. He was then able to bring her in under control for a further attempt and subsequently took off some wounded soldiers and prisoners.

Private Grant was so badly wounded in the stomach that Private Scott 335 had to shout and scream at him to keep moving

ALC *138* during training. It is possible Able Seaman Burns is the rating standing above 'A4'.

to an ALC. Scott believed he was the last aboard. The ALC moved off too quickly and took on water up to their knees, forcing them to use a hand pump and bale with their helmets. It was difficult to transfer CSM Strachan from the ALC to a MGB and Scott and Lance Corporal Fleming had to manhandle him, Strachan all the while shouting for a drink.

The skipper of ALC *135*, Sub-Lieutenant R J F Turner, jumped into the water with a rope under fire to steady his craft and encourage some paratroopers to get aboard. With fourteen men loaded he shoved off, but another man was sighted and he went in again to pick him up, once more jumping into the water to control the craft. On ALC *138* the Coxswain, Able Seaman W D Burns, managed to get twenty men aboard in difficult sea conditions while shipping a large quantity of water.

When the prisoners and wounded had been taken off, the remainder of the force embarked. Cook had to use a megaphone to be heard over the firing, but some men were more aware of the enemy fire than others; Cox described it as slight and soon silenced by the Brens in the boats.

Frost ordered the rearguard to fall back to the beach. With a counter-attack looming, the last of the raiders were taken off. At 0315 just as mortar bombs and grenades began to fall from above, a call was shouted for any men on the beach to board the last landing craft. There was no response and the boat set off; Frost was the last man aboard. This boat loitered a short while to see if anyone else turned up, then set off to join the others.

Two boats had to be towed away, including ALC *134* with the burned out engines, and another seriously overloaded. The number of men taken off by each landing craft varied; one left overloaded with fifty initially while another left with just one man aboard. The post-raid medical report is the only one that breaks down the number taken off by each craft:

LSC *1*	Unspecified number from overcrowded ALC *3*
LSC 2	Twenty from the overcrowded ALC *3*
ALC *3* (*134*)	Fifty
ALC *4* (*135*)	Fifteen including three casualties
ALC 5	Twelve including three casualties
ALC *6*	One who had fallen into the sea
ALC *7*	A number of raiders including three casualties, one being a prisoner
ALC *8*	Five

MGB *312* towing two ALCs during training.

It is known ALC *125* took off some prisoners and ALC *138* took off twenty raiders, but it has not been possible to identify which craft these were, although the strongest candidate for ALC *138* appears to be ALC *7*. Given two men were killed ashore and six men were left behind, the total taken off the beach was 112. From the figures above about eighty-three were recovered by five ALCs, leaving ALC *7* with the balance of twenty-nine.

In the darkness the captured radar parts and twenty men transferred from ALC *134* to MGB *312*. Preist climbed aboard the MGB first and told the men on the ALC to hand the radar parts up to him as he leaned over the rail. It seemed that when the swell pushed him up, the ALC went down, but eventually the precious cargo was transferred and the MGB raced off at 20 knots.

Once aboard MGB *312*, Cox wanted to be seasick, but Preist envisaged him being unable to remember anything if he allowed him to slip into a daze in his exhausted state, 'Sorry, old man. Come down below and tell me the story. Then you can be sick.' Cox gave his report very clearly, then went on deck and was violently ill. He managed to get down a strong cup of tea and then fell asleep in the skipper's bunk with Corporal Jones.

The eight landing craft did not have the range to make it back to England under their own power and by 0320 they had been taken in tow in tandem by the other four MGBs. By 0326 all raiders had been transferred to the MGBs, leaving just the naval crews and fire support teams aboard the landing craft. With the wind increasing to Force 5 and the MGBs only able to make seven knots while towing, it was a miserable experience in the small boats en route home. Tows parted twice and had to be replaced. Seasickness was rife. One German was badly affected and spent a long time hanging over the rail of a MGB with his leg held in a vice like grip by a little paratrooper. When asked by Cook why he was doing this he replied, 'Sirr, I've come all this way to get a Hun prisoner and I'm damned if I'm going to let this bastard get awa' the noo!'

The French submarine chaser *Larmor* (CH 42).

HMS *Fernie* – both she and HMS *Blencathra* were Hunt Class destroyers.

By dawn they were only fifteen miles from the French coast, but the journey back was uneventful. The force was escorted by four Free French *chasseurs* (light destroyers or submarine chasers), the *Bayonne, Calais, Larmor* and *La Lavandou,* from twenty-five miles southeast of the EA5 rescue float. At 0815 a flight of Spitfires arrived and later two British destroyers (HMS *Fernie* and *Blencathra*), joined them.

The two signalers missing from NELSON (Privates Embury and Cornell) were amongst those left behind. The naval signaler on Frost's MGB received a message saying they had reached the beach, but it was too late as the evacuation force had already departed. Frost despaired, but Cook rightly would not risk returning for them.

E-boat (enemy boat) known as S-Boot (*Schnellboot*) to the Germans were capable of 40-50 knots.

A German destroyer of the period; it is not known which ships were active off Bruneval on the night of the raid.

Over rum below deck in the warmth of the MGBs the Navy explained why they had been delayed. Two German destroyers and two E- or R-boats had passed within a mile to seaward of them. They moved on when a red navigation light was switched on at Le Havre. Fortunately the moon was to seaward of the German ships, and with the British vessels in darkness against the land, they were not spotted. The Germans had illuminated the lighthouse to assist this small flotilla and Cook had made a lucky decision when he moved the landing craft close to shore earlier than planned. Had he not, the Germans ships would have steamed straight into them. All thirteen boats cut their engines and bobbed up and down praying to be overlooked. They had no torpedoes and were powerless to take on the destroyers. It is likely the attention of the German ships was diverted by the raid near Le Havre and the flashes from the fighting at Bruneval. Fortunately the flares fired by the beach garrison came a little later, or they may have silhouetted Cook's small flotilla.

Frost, unlike many, was an excellent sailor and tucked into an early breakfast in the finest traditions of the senior service. While eating, a message was received from Preist on MGB *312*, 'Samples complete and perfect'. At 0815, Cook signaled Commander-in-Chief Portsmouth the codeword 'Maple' meaning the operation had been successful, the radar parts had been embarked and all boats were on their way home. MGB *312* arrived at HMS *Prins Albert* off Spithead at 1010 and the captured equipment was unloaded at 1130.

Some of the medics on the other MGBs were kept busy with casualties. From the post-raid medical report, it is known nine were considered serious enough to warrant morphine, including

Royal Naval Hospital Haslar. It closed in 2009 having been the site of a naval hospital since 1753.

one of the prisoners and a man with a head wound who was rather excitable at first (Corporal Stewart). At Portsmouth three were taken to the sick bay on HMS *Prins Albert* before being transferred to Haslar Naval Hospital at Gosport and four more were taken directly to Haslar by the MGBs. Other injuries were less severe, for example two landing craft crewmen and one raider, who fell down a cliff, suffered minor abrasions. Those casualties requiring hospital treatment were:

Sergeant J Boyd – gun shot wound left foot
Private W Grant – gun shot wound abdomen
Lance Corporal R Heard – gun shot wound left hand
Corporal G Heslop – gun shot wound left thigh
Private H Shaw – gun shot wound left leg
Corporal V Stewart – gun shot wound scalp
CSM G Strachan – gun shot wound abdomen

Stoker C W Hurst on ALC *134* volunteered to carry out repairs on the two engines. Despite working in very cramped conditions in the fume filled engine room and being tossed up and down in the swell, he managed to get both running again during the journey home.

Charteris spent much of the journey back chatting with his prisoner, Corporal Schmidt. Most men tried to sleep in the bobbing boats with little success, but sea conditions improved as they entered the Solent. At 1530 the landing craft were cast off from the MGBs and, under their own power, rejoined HMS *Prins*

The ALCs approaching HMS *Prins Albert*.

Having been winched aboard HMS *Prins Albert*, a fire support team disembarks from an ALC, to be greeted by a crowd of naval, military and air force personnel.

An MGB carrying a party of raiders edges alongside HMS *Prins Albert*. Frost is on the left of the bridge. Group Captain Norman (head framed in the circular antenna) has boarded for the final part of the journey.

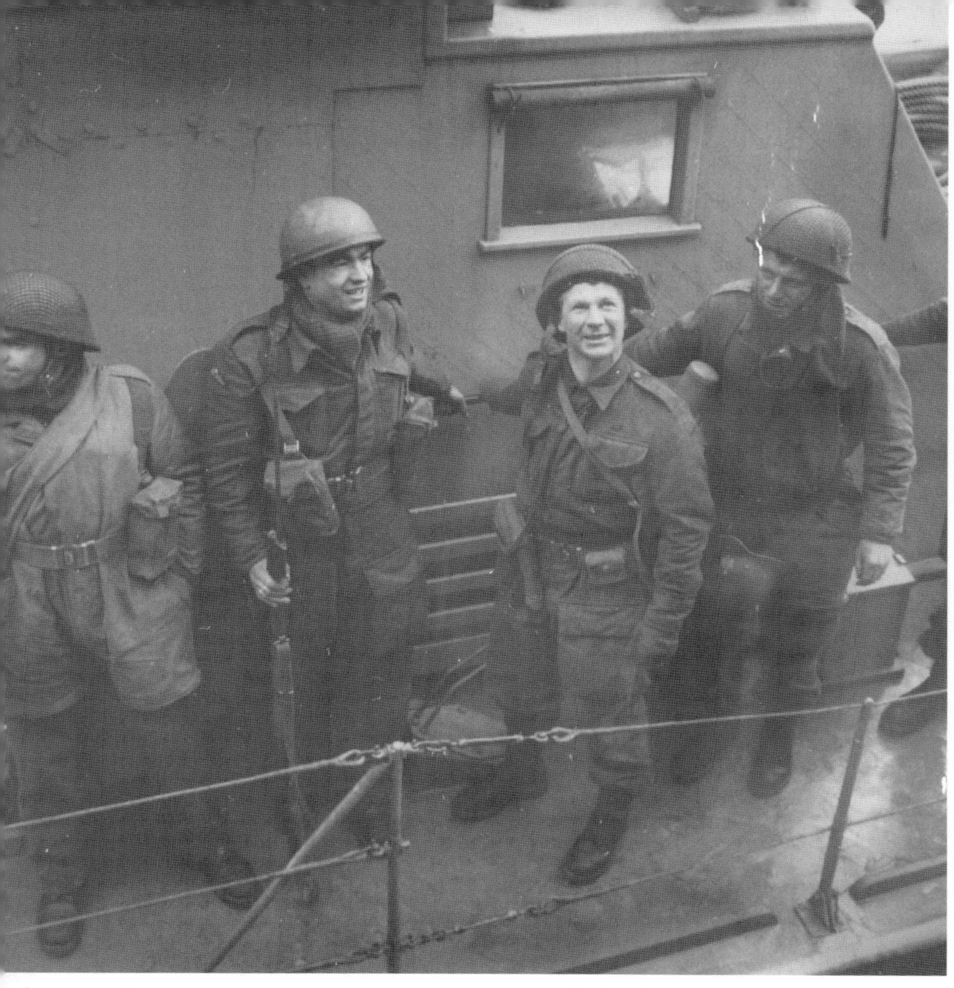

A group of paratroopers waiting to disembark from a MGB. The man with fixed bayonet appears in other pictures. The man on the right has a German helmet attached to his belt. It appears in other pictures and is now in the Airborne Forces Museum at Duxford.

Albert around 1635 to be winched aboard. Despite everything he achieved later, Frost remembered the arrival in the sheltered waters of the Solent, standing on the bridge of the MGB, as one of the moments never to be forgotten. The French and British destroyers swept by in salute, the latter playing 'Rule Britannia' over their loudhailers, and the escorting Spitfires swooped low overhead in salute before heading inland for their base.

On board HMS *Prins Albert* they received a tremendous welcome. Pickard and many of his aircrew were there, amongst

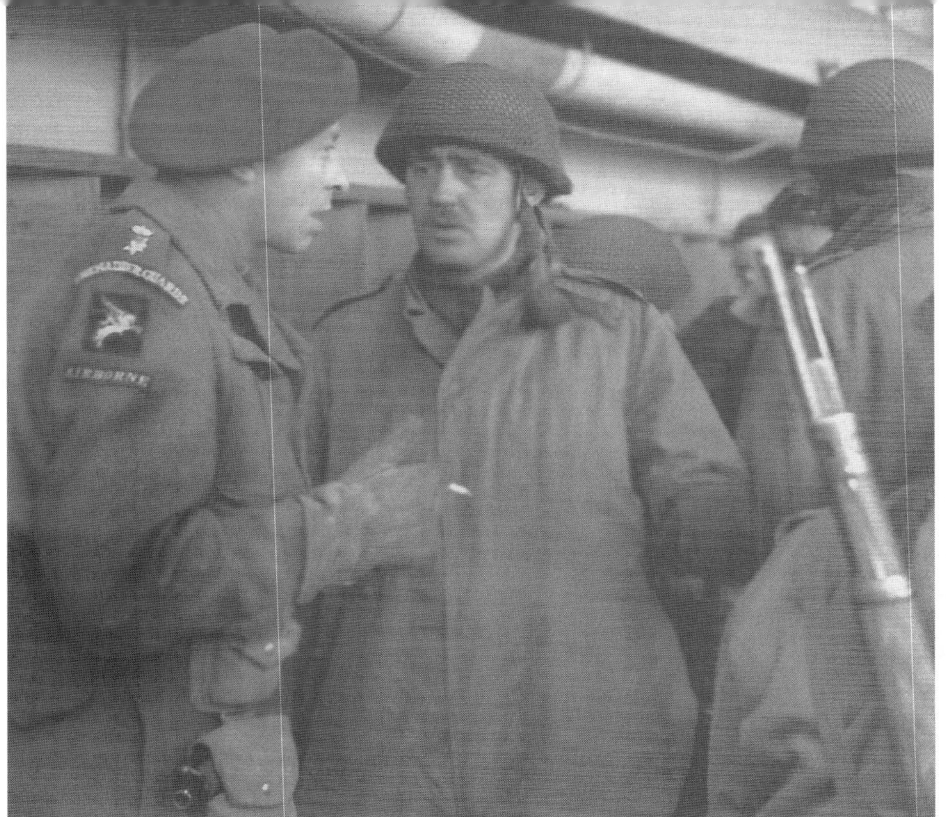

A serious looking Major Frost in conversation with Lieutenant Colonel Johnny Goschen, Assistant Adjutant and Quartermaster General HQ Airborne Division, on the deck of HMS *Prins Albert*. Note the German Mauser rifle barrel.

a large group of staff officers, photographers and reporters. That evening there was a tri-service party in the Naval Mess resulting in monumental headaches.

Cook replied to Mountbatten's eve of raid signal:

> *Your inspiring message received pm Friday 27 Feb 1942 was much appreciated by all. Boche Bitten!*

Opposite: Group Captain Norman (righ chats with Flight Sergeant Cox (centr and Corporal Jones on HMS *Prins Albe* Cox has folded his parachute smo under his arm. This picture was probab taken just after MGB *312* arrived in th morning, ahead of the arrival of the ma force on the afternoon of 28 Februa

Pickard examines the German helmet in a posed press photograph – the man with the bayonet is there.

Corporal Schmidt is brought aboard HMS *Prins Albert* and handed over to local security troops.

Private Tewes on the left with the bandage around his neck and the Luftwaffe prisoner are searched again aboard HMS *Prins Albert* for the benefit of the cameras.

Chapter Ten

RESULTS OF THE RAID

THE MORALE EFFECT of the raid was out of all proportion to its size. The success was splashed across the British press and went some way towards improving morale after a string of failures, including the fall of Singapore and the failure to stop the Channel Dash by *Scharnhorst*, *Gneisenau* and *Prinz Eugen* two weeks earlier. It also gave the French hope. Lord Haw Haw referred scathingly to the raiders as a 'handful of redskins', but press coverage in America was positive, helping keep alive the notion that Britain was not beaten and could strike back.

How the *Evening Standard* reported the raid – this is probably the paper Cox referred to late on 1 March when he told his family where he had been.

FINAL NIGHT EXTRA

Evening Standard

BLACK-OUT: 7.1 pm.—7.11 am.

ONE PENNY

No. 36,654 LONDON SATURDAY, FEBRUARY 28, 1942

OLIVER
For POWER EFFICIENCY and SPEED

KING SIX CIGARS 8d each

British Paratroops, Followed Up by Infantry, Wreck the Nazis Radio "Eyes" Across Channel

ARMY, NAVY & RAF RAID N. FRANCE IN THE DARK

"It Was to Schedule and Very Successful"

In a combined operation, joint forces of the Royal Navy, of the Army and of the R.A.F. successfully attacked an important radio location post on the north coast of France.

THIS WAS ANNOUNCED TO-DAY BY THE ADMIRALTY, WAR OFFICE AND THE AIR MINISTRY IN A JOINT COMMUNIQUE, WHICH ADDED:

"Parachute troops of an airborne division were dropped by bombers of the R.A.F.

"The task was finished according to schedule and the parachute troops were supported in the latter half of their task by infantry and are being brought back by the Royal Navy."

First reports received in London to-day indicate that the raid was "very successful."

The operation was carried out to a strict time schedule dictated by the hours of darkness available. The paratroops were preceded by bombers and night fighters, which attacked airfields and gun posts. Their withdrawal was covered on land by the supporting infantry and from the sea by light naval craft. The R.A.F. maintained offensive patrols over the area until all the troops had been withdrawn.

It was stated that while the operation was a spectacular one, it must be regarded as small. Although reference is made to a combined operation, it did not necessarily mean that Commandos were used.

COAL TO BE RATIONED ON MONDAY

Evening Standard Reporter

Coal will be rationed in London on Monday.

You will be restricted to a total of six cwt for the six weeks beginning on that day—one cwt a week—if you live in the London Civil Defence Region, which is approximately the same as the Metropolitan Police area.

This comprises the City of London, the 28 Metropolitan boroughs, the county boroughs of Croydon, East and West Ham, the County of Middlesex, and parts of Hertfordshire, Essex, Kent and Surrey.

You will not be supplied with coal during the next six weeks if you have more than half a ton already in stock on Monday.

The order will not apply to boiler fuel or coke.

700 STRIKE AT SMITHFIELD

About 700 Smithfield porters and warehousemen to-day continued a strike which began yesterday afternoon.

They are the employees of a number of merchants at the market. A member of one of the firms said: "The strike is not

JAP INVASION FLEET FLEES FROM JAVA

THE BIGGEST NAVAL BATTLE OF THE FAR EASTERN WAR RAGED THROUGHOUT MOST OF YESTERDAY AND TO-DAY IN THE JAVA SEA BETWEEN THE SOUTH COAST OF BORNEO AND SURABAYA, THE ALLIES' GREAT NAVAL BASE.

Although the raid was widely publicized, mention of its true objective was not revealed until after the war. One officer, one non-commissioned officer and one private were allowed to describe the operation in full to the press, but were not to mention that radar equipment was brought back. Frost recorded an interview for the BBC, but the Ministry of Information would not allow it to be broadcast.

The day after the raid, a Hurricane approached Bruneval undetected and flew over the radar pit before the Germans could react. It then machine-gunned a group of officers examining the damaged installation, causing them to dive for cover. A few days later proof of the success came when a force of bombers flew over the site unmolested to bomb the Renault munitions factory in Paris.

Combined Operations had put together an ambitious, but highly successful operation involving all three services and thereby gained considerable experience. The raid proved the military importance of a small and highly trained group of men and the impact they could have. It confirmed airborne operations were a viable way of striking at 'Fortress Europe' and prompted the War Office to expand airborne forces. An Airborne Forces Depot and Battle School were set up at Hardwick in Derbyshire in April 1942 when 1st Parachute Brigade moved out. The Parachute Regiment was created on 1 August 1942 and Bruneval is its first battle honour, although it occurred five months before its formation. A number of infantry battalions converted to the airborne role in August 1942 and over the next two years airborne forces expanded to two divisions in Europe. RAF lift capacity increased enormously to carry them.

Badge of the Parachute Regiment.

The Luftwaffe prisoner brought back from Bruneval. Unfortunately his name is not known. The tear in his tunic is where Peter Nagel ripped off a badge.

The *Luftwaffe* prisoner was more than willing to talk having been imprisoned by his own side for twenty months of the war. He had been conscripted into the *Luftwaffe* in April 1939 and received basic infantry and Morse training at Augsburg, although he could not cope with the latter. In September 1939 he applied for compassionate leave to visit his sick child and, when it was refused, went absent. He was arrested at home and a few days later the child died. He was sent to prison for six months. A week after being released, leave was again refused and he went on a two-day party in Augsburg instead. His sentence this time was twelve months, plus two months remitted from his first sentence for good behaviour. He served his time in Munich, Torgau and the VW factory at Fallersleben. When released in April 1941 he carried on working at the factory until September, when he was sent to France and spent a few days in a number of units before joining the unit at Étretat.

He had been at the radar site since November 1941, which is where he was trained. He admitted he was not as competent as some operators who would have been of more help, but the British had shot them. He was not very bright, as he believed that somehow the radar 'saw' aircraft and was therefore not as effective in poor weather. However, he was able to explain how the system worked and his presence compensated for the lack of display equipment, with which he was familiar.

R V Jones and his team spent an afternoon sitting on the floor with the prisoner, surrounded by the recovered equipment before it went for detailed technical examination at TRE. They learned the *Freya* warned the *Würzburg* by telephone to switch on and look on a particular bearing, as *Würzburg* could only scan an arc of 5%. The *Würzburg* operator turned the dish with a handle and tilted it until maximum response from the target was gained. Having obtained range, bearing and altitude the operator passed this to a local plotting centre. The prisoner related how on one occasion the flak in Le Havre fired blindly at an object he had reported high in the sky, then looked outside and realized it was a ship. Despite the operator's lack of finesse, the station claimed to have participated in the destruction of sixty-four aircraft and two ships. Jones deduced that due to its method of operation alone, *Würzburg* could be out-manoeuvred quite easily.

The prisoner had a bizarre theory as to what prompted the raid. A month earlier he had been on leave and mentioned to his wife that the Bruneval site was so exposed the British could easily launch a raid against it. Having told her about this, he

Front of the *Würzburg* transmitter recovered from Bruneval.

The Bruneval modulator unit, with the small cathode ray tube screen used for calibration purposes in the centre.

The mixer unit.

Intermediate frequency strip from the *Würzburg*. This was known to be in the Brenzett Aeronautical Museum in 1982, but has since disappeared.

Two of the unique markings on the recovered *Würzburg* parts. Where are these important historical items now?

wondered whether his wife was a British spy.

The dismantling party returned with the receiver, receiver amplifier, modulator (timing control), transmitter and the antenna element. Only the display equipment (cathode ray tube) was left behind due to lack of time. From the recovered pieces and the prisoner, TRE rebuilt the *Würzburg* and was able to determine a great deal.

From analysis of the metal manufacturer's plates, they learned *Würzburg* was produced by Telefunken near Berlin. From the serial numbers it was apparent there were at least 1093 items. The earliest equipment inspection was early November 1940 on the transmitter and the latest August 1941 on the antenna. About 500 sets had been produced and the rate of

Luftwaffe General Wolfgang Martini. His interest in radio started at school. He was a military communicator throughout the First World War and remained in the small post-war Army until transferring to the newly formed *Luftwaffe* in 1933. Martini saw the value of radar from the first demonstration and was instrumental in introducing it into *Luftwaffe* service. He had frequent disagreements with Göring about the effectiveness of British radar. When the new *Luftwaffe* formed in 1956 he returned to service and became very friendly with Robert Watson-Watt, 'the father of British radar'.

production was about 100 per month.

Würzburg was not very sophisticated, being simple in principle, but it was engineered to a high standard. Its components were modular, which made faultfinding and maintenance simpler than on British models. This was confirmed during the interrogation of the operator, who provided valuable information about operator skills and training, but proved to be less well trained than his British counterparts. After the war R V Jones asked General Martini, Head of *Luftwaffe Signals and Radar*, why the equipment was so well engineered, but the operators had comparatively low technical ability. Martini explained it was because he had such a low priority for manpower. There was little expertise available anyway, because the Nazis had banned amateur radio. So they ensured the equipment was well made and easily replaceable to compensate for relatively unskilled per-sonnel.

Würzburg could only track one aircraft at a time, unless two were on a very similar bearing and elevation, which confirmed Jones' theory on how the Germans night-fighter defences were organized. By then it was known that the *Würzburg Riese* existed and, as it used a larger spinning antenna, would be even more accurate. Jones believed this larger version was the main opposition for British bombers, as it would control the night fighters. However, its components were essentially the same as those recovered from Bruneval; they had what they needed.

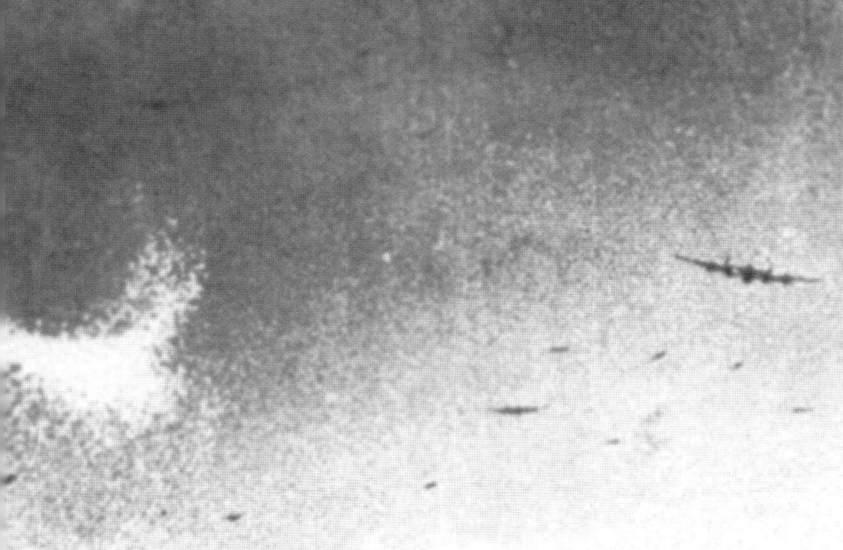

A cloud of Window released by a force of Lancasters during a raid over Germany.

The left side of this *Würzburg* screen has been obliterated by Window. The small blip on the right is what an operator would expect to see from an individual aircraft.

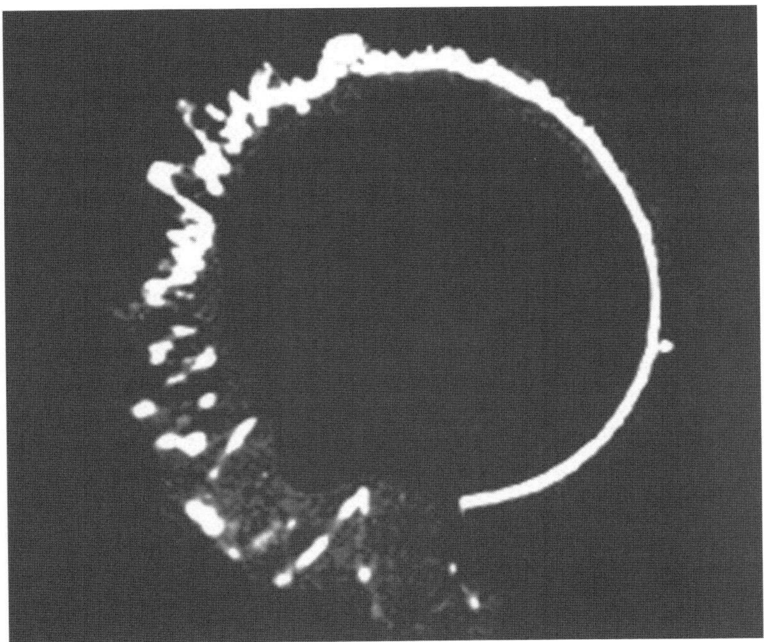

Würzburg had a range of about forty kilometres and was tunable over a wide range making it impervious to jamming by conventional means available to the British at the time. However, 'Window' or chaff (small pieces of metal foil released from aircraft) would blind the quality of operator captured at Bruneval. Both sides, believing themselves to be ahead in the radar war, thought they had the most to lose by using Window and held back. Göring even refused to hear the German codename, *Düppel,* uttered in senior meetings. The British refrained from using Window for seventeen months, but Bomber Command's raids on Hamburg in July 1943 confirmed its effectiveness against *Würzburg.* All the air defence radars were blinded and the operators were utterly confused, being unable to distinguish between a bomber and several pieces of Window giving off a similar signature. Similarly the Allies were able to jam *Würzburg* very successfully ahead of the D-Day landings.

Chapter Eleven

THE AFTERMATH

THE GERMANS patrolled the area around Bruneval on 28 February, looking for 'commandos', unsure if the raid had been a cover to infiltrate large numbers for other tasks. They initially had four prisoners; one wounded (Private Sutherland) and three unwounded (Lance Corporal MacCullam and Privates Thomas and Willoughby). The unwounded prisoners were taken to the Hotel Beauminet for initial questioning in English. Everything appears to have been done properly and the British troops were in good spirits; Madame Vennier saw them laughing and joking. Two dead Germans lay under blankets for two days under the ping-pong table in the dining room.

Three days later the Gestapo arrived and accused the Venniers of harbouring an Englishman, which was ridiculous as the hotel was crawling with German soldiers. After several other fruitless lines of questioning they left, but a few days later a *Leutnant* moved into one of the rooms and arrived at all hours of day and night, probably planted by the Gestapo to catch them out.

Lance Corporal MacCullam and Privates Thomas and Willoughby being held at the Hotel Beauminet shortly after the raid.

The picture on the previous page was taken outside the building on the right at the rear of the Hotel, which is now a private house.

Dining room of the Hotel pre-war.

Lance Corporal MacCullam and Privates Thomas and Willoughby in German custody, believed to be in Étratat – Sutherland would have been in hospital and Embury and Cornell were still at large.

The Germans set up a new *Würzburg* in the *Freya* compound at Bruneval and demolished the chateau, because it was a conspicuous landmark, but the cellar was retained and converted into a shelter. The Germans conveniently surrounded all coastal radar sites with barbed wire, making them very distinctive from the air, particularly when grass grew up through the wire. During the costly Dieppe Raid in August 1942, a subsidiary mission to capture *Freya* components failed, largely because of these new defences. However, visibility from the air made them easier to target and neutralise prior to D-Day in June 1944.

The German after action report admitted they failed to stop the raiders infiltrating between Hill 102 and Bruneval and subsequently reaching the beach. However, they believed their actions prevented the raiders reaching the *Freya*. Frost's orders allowed him this option, but only if the *Würzburg* parts had been recovered, there was no significant opposition and there was time before the evacuation. No such attempt was made.

With the parachute force landing in two places, it masked the true objective and the Germans did not head en masse for the chateau, where they might have been used more decisively. However, the immediate actions taken by the Germans prevented a number of raiders getting to the beach who were subsequently taken prisoner. The report commented, 'The operation of the British Commandos was well planned and executed with great discipline... Although attacked by German soldiers they concentrated on their primary task.' They were particularly impressed with one party's discipline, as it did not open fire for at least thirty minutes. This was almost certainly DRAKE or RODNEY.

The British estimated up to forty enemy were killed, but German sources admit only five fatalities. The Army had two killed, one seriously wounded and two missing (presumably the two prisoners taken to England). The *Luftwaffe* had three killed, one wounded and three missing (presumably this included the radar operator prisoner). The same German report recorded the British dead and prisoners accurately, so it seems likely the German casualty estimates were correct.

For the British the operation was a spectacular success. Losses were comparatively light – two dead, seven returned with serious wounds and six were missing, including one wounded; all of the missing were eventually captured and survived the war. The two dead, Rifleman Hugh Duncan McDonald McIntyre and Private Alan Worton Scott are buried side by side in Ste Marie Cemetery, Le Havre, France. Initial British reports concluded the raid came as a surprise to the Germans. The defences were not as strong as expected and the troops encountered were either very young or elderly and easily surprised. The defenders used a great deal of tracer ammunition, but tended to fire high and wildly.

The two RODNEY signalers, who reached the beach after the rest of the force had been evacuated (Privates Embury and Cornell), moved inland and evaded the advancing Germans. They sheltered in a barn at Le Tilleul until daylight, when the fifteen-year-old son of the farmer saw them from the house. He

The graves of Private A W Scott Royal Berkshire Regiment and Rifleman H D McD McIntyre The Cameronians in Ste Marie Cemetery, Le Havre (Division 67, Row E, Graves 3 & 4). Both gravestones incorrectly show they were attached to the Parachute Regiment, which did not form for five months after their deaths.

Division 67, one of the Commonwealth War Graves Commission Second World W plots in Ste Marie Cemetery, Le Havre.

Bekanntmachung
Sehr wichtig !

Es liegt Veranlassung vor, nochmals auf die Bekanntmachung des Militärbefehlshabers in Frankreich vom 2.8.1941 hinzuweisen, die folgenden Wortlaut hat :

« Jeder Landeseinwohner, der Angehörigen englischer Flugzeugbesatzungen zur Flucht verhilft oder auch nur den Versuch dazu macht oder diese sonst irgendwie unterstützt, wird unverzüglich vor ein deutsches Kriegsgericht gestellt und mit dem Tode bestraft ».

2. August 1941. DER MILITÄRBEFEHLSHABER IN FRANKREICH.

Unter Flugzeugbesatzung sind auch abgesprungene Fallschirmjäger zu verstehen.

Le Havre, den 2. März 1942.

DER KREISKOMMANDANT

AVIS
TRÈS IMPORTANT

Je me vois dans la nécessité d'appuyer, encore une fois, sur l'ordonnance du Militaerbefehlshaber in Frankreich du 2 Août 1941, dont le texte est le suivant :

« Quiconque aiderait des aviateurs anglais descendus en territoire français à s'enfuir, leur prêterait son concours ou leur prêterait assistance, de n'importe quelle manière, serait transféré immédiatement devant la cour martiale allemande *et puni de mort* ».

Le 2 Août 1941 DER MILITAERBEFEHLSHABER IN FRANKREICH

On entend aussi par aviateurs les parachutistes anglais descendus en territoire français.

Le Havre, le 2 Mars 1942.

DER KREISKOMMANDANT

German notice of 2 March 1942 reminding the French population that the penalty for helping the British was death.

spoke no English and they only a few words of French. The family would be in serious trouble if caught harbouring the enemy, but they took them in and gave them hot soup and calvados. It was snowing and if the soldiers moved they would be easy to track. The mother spoke a little English and said they could hide in the attic until the Resistance could help.

They were sheltered by Maurice de la Joie and his wife and then by his sister, Madame Delarue, for a few days. Having been given civilian clothing and Belgian papers, they got on a train with the de la Joies and were well on their way to Switzerland. On leaving the train at the Demarcation Line at Blere, Indre-et-Loire on 9 March they were arrested by the Germans. Their stories didn't ring true and they were taken to Paris for questioning about their part in the raid and the French who helped them. Eventually they were classed as prisoners of war and sent to Lamsdorf (*Stalag VIII-B*).

The de la Joies were condemned to death by a German military tribunal at Angers and imprisoned in Paris, he at Cherche-Midi and she at La Santé.

The barn at Le Tilleul in which Embury and Cornell hid immediately after the raid.

In January 1943 they were sent to Breslau in Silesia; she ended up in Ravensbrück and he in Buchenwald. Both survived the war, but as invalids.

The morning after getting back, Preist and Bromley-Martin went to the Air Ministry to meet CAS, Air Marshal Sir Charles Portal, who was pleased at the success of the raid. The same morning, Cox also reported to the Air Ministry to see Air Commodore Tait, who sent him on two weeks leave. Cox asked Tait's Women's Auxiliary Air Force secretary to telegram his family in Wisbech, 'Home tonight kill the fatted calf.' It was midnight before he walked in to be greeted by four generations of his family sitting around the fire. Cox said, 'Hullo family, I've been in France, that's where I've been, and it's in the London newspapers tonight. How about that then?'

Agent Remy's Lysander landed at Tangmere and he was taken to London where he was put up in the Waldorf. Later that day he was briefed on the success of the raid and was so exuberant he drafted a message to fellow agent Pol, 'Congratulations success Bruneval which has resulted destruction important German installation while taking and killing numerous Boches.' Remy was to regret this. It was the last time his old code was used. The Germans broke it and used it to identify Pol who was executed a year later at Mont-Valérien.

C Company returned to Tilshead very late on 28 February and spent 1 March resting and cleaning themselves and their weapons and equipment. Browning visited the wounded in hospital the same day.

At 2100 on 2 March, Churchill assembled members of the War Cabinet and Chiefs of Staff to hear about the raid. Present were Attlee (Deputy Prime Minister), Eden (Foreign Secretary), Grigg (War Office), Alexander (Admiralty), Sinclair (Air), Lyttleton (Production), Pound (1st Sea Lord), Brooke (Chief of Imperial General Staff), Portal (CAS), Mountbatten, Browning and Wing Commander The Marquis de Casa Maury (Senior Intelligence Officer at HQ Combined Ops).

Modern entrance to the Cabinet War Rooms below the Treasury with King Charles Street beyond leading to Whitehall.

Frost had been about to slip into a bath at Tilshead when he got a call to get to London immediately. He had not even had time to conduct a full debrief with all participants by then. He was taken to the War Cabinet rooms under the current Treasury building, where the briefing model had been set up. Mountbatten gave the main briefing. At one point Eden and Sinclair were having a private conversation in a corner. Churchill halted Mountbatten, told the two to listen as they might learn something for once and then had Mountbatten continue. Frost briefed his part and then answered Churchill's question about the quality of information received before the raid, very positively. Churchill told him he was standing next to the man responsible, Casa Maury. Churchill then asked CAS what he hoped to gain from the captured equipment. The technical details went over his head and he had to ask Portal to keep it simple. At the end Churchill was elated and demanded more raids. As a result Mountbatten and Browning instantly harangued CAS for more aircraft. Frost left for his club and a delayed bath.

Wing Commander The Marquis de Casa Maury, Senior Intelligence Officer at HQ Combined Operations – he was a racing car driver and founder of Curzon Cinema in Mayfair in 1934.

Frost came back to earth soon after when Army bureaucracy began asking questions about items of equipment left behind in France. He returned to Hardwick on 5 March and went on leave before undertaking a lecture tour of various units and HQs,

King George VI and Queen Elizabeth watch a parachute demonstration at Dishforth. Frost stands between them and Pickard is on the right of the Queen.

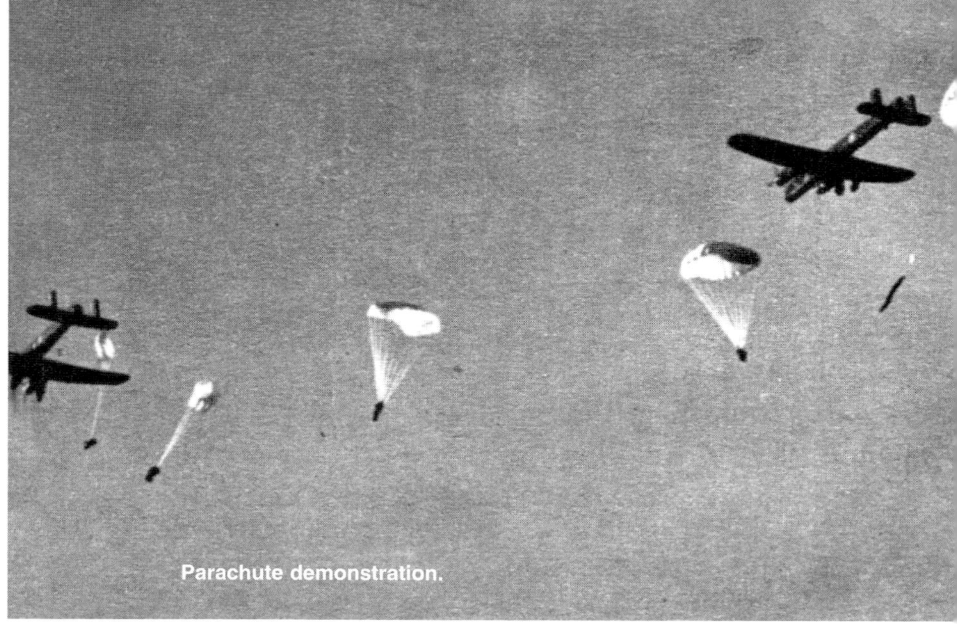
Parachute demonstration.

including HQ US 8th Air Force and the Polish Parachute Brigade. On 28 March, Lieutenant Charteris and Sergeants McKenzie and Campbell went on a PR tour in support of the Ministry of Supply until 3 April. On 31 March, Frost lectured 21 (Training) Group RAF at Cranwell on airborne operations.

The King requested a demonstration of a parachute drop. This took place at Dishforth and was carried out by 51 Squadron and a company of 3rd Parachute Battalion with Frost in attendance. It was arranged that the first aircraft would approach the airfield as their Majesties arrived at the main gate. Unfortunately, the King decided to inspect the Guardroom and there was a mad scramble to hold back the aircraft, but ten dropped their loads before they could be stopped. The demonstration was not as spectacular with only twenty paratroopers descending instead of 120. Afterwards in the Mess the King asked why there were black footprints on the ceiling. Pickard told his Majesty they were the result of his feet being covered in boot polish and being laid on top of piled up furniture to leave his mark. When the King noticed two large black blobs, Pickard had to admit they were the imprints of his buttocks. Fortunately the King burst out laughing. Clearly the post-Bruneval party had been a good one.

On 15 May 1942 a special supplement to the *London Gazette* announced eighteen decorations:

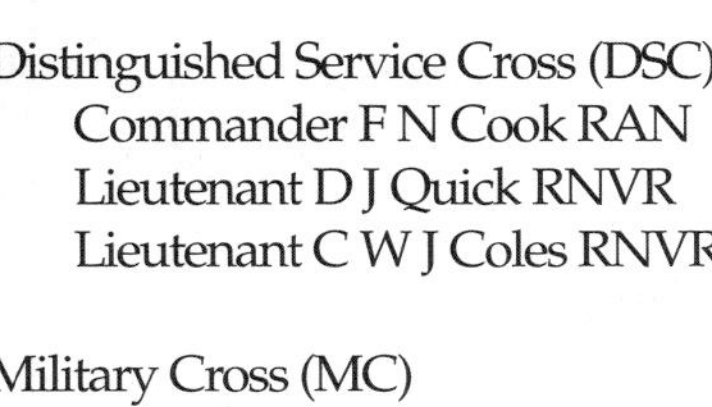

DSC

Distinguished Service Cross (DSC)
- Commander F N Cook RAN
- Lieutenant D J Quick RNVR
- Lieutenant C W J Coles RNVR

MC

Military Cross (MC)
- Major J D Frost Cameronians
- Lieutenant E B C Charteris KOSB

Distinguished Service Medal (DSM)
- Able Seaman J T Bland
- Stoker C W Hurst

DSM

Military Medal (MM)
- Flight Sergeant C W H Cox RAF
- Sergeant G McKenzie Black Watch
- Sergeant D Grieve Seaforth Highlanders

MM

Mentioned in Despatches (MID)
- Lieutenant P A Young East Surrey
- Lieutenant Commander W G Everitt RN
- Lieutenant Commander H B Peate RNR
- Lieutenant Commander G H Garrard RNVR
- Lieutenant PR Mackinnon RNVR
- Sub-Lieutenant R J F Turner RNVR
- Chief Motor Mechanic B Barry
- Able Seaman W D Burns.

MID

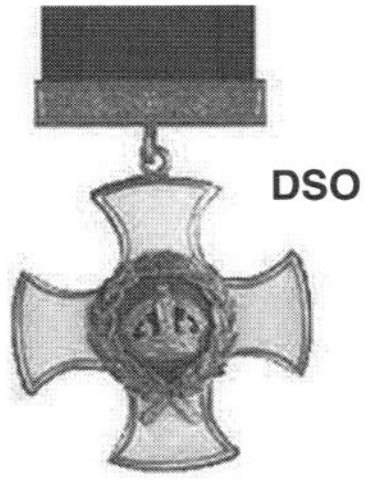

DSO

Pickard was awarded a Bar to his Distinguished Service Order (DSO) on 26 May. CSM Strachan received the French Croix de Guerre with Palm in January 1944. Chief Motor Mechanic Barry also later received the Croix de Guerre with Vermilion Star.

Fears grew of a retaliatory raid on TRE Worth. German interest in the site increased and British reconnaissance photographs proved the parabolic dishes there could be seen from six miles away. Air attacks became more frequent and in one raid a number of RAF airmen were killed. There were reports of German paratroopers massing near Cherbourg and an infantry battalion was drafted in to

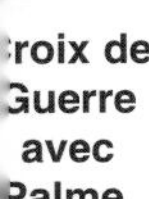

roix de Guerre avec Palme.

Walls are all that remain of the Worth Matravers Chain Home Low station.

provide extra protection. Whatever the truth, TRE had grown enormously and was vital for the development of all forms of radar. From Cherbourg the Germans could monitor transmissions while new equipment was being trialed. TRE needed to move in order to get on with the war in peace. Churchill ordered it out of Worth Matravers before the next full moon. On 26 May 1942, TRE transferred to Malvern (its successor organization is still there). TRE Worth only existed for twenty-two months, but the work carried out there was irreplaceable. All that remains today are the ruins of a Chain Home Low station and a memorial in the shape of a radar dish overlooking the sea at St Aldhelm's Head:

> *This Memorial Commemorates The Radar Research Carried Out At Worth Matravers From 1940 – 1942 Which Was Crucial To The Winning Of The War And The Birth Of Modern Telecommunications.*

R V Jones studied the *Himmelbett* air defence system, taking into account the results of the technical examination of the *Würzburg* and the *Luftwaffe* prisoner's testimony on how it was used. He

Memorial at St Aldhelm's Head to the work carried out by TRE Worth 1940-42, with the ancient chapel and coastguard station in the background.

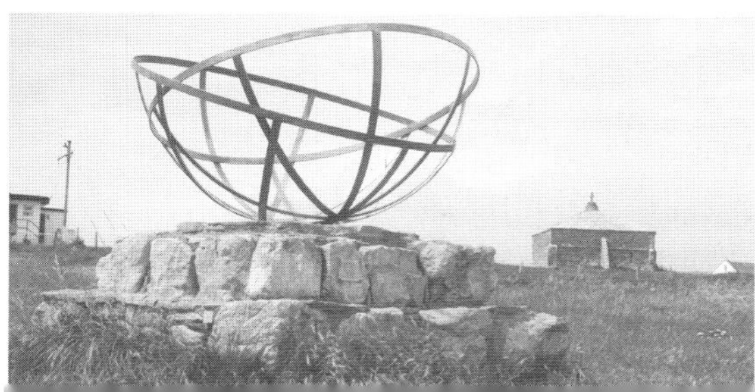

realised that with only one night fighter operating in each box, flying all RAF bombers through just one of them could saturate the air defences. Thus began the bomber stream, which was used for the first time most successfully on the first 1,000 Bomber raid on Cologne 30/31 May 1942.

In early 1944, *Generalfeldmarschall* Rommel and his staff visited Bruneval to inspect the coastal defences, following which they had cognac in the road outside the Hotel. Next day the order came to evacuate all civilians. The Venniers left the Hotel on 15 February, never to return. Numerous new defences were built in the area, many around features that played a part in the raid. On 4 June 1944, dive-bombers destroyed two key radar stations just prior to the Normandy landings. Of the 120 men who parachuted into Bruneval, 112 returned to Britain. Of these, 14 were killed (12.5%) in other actions before the end of the war: in North Africa 11; Sicily 1; Arnhem 2 (where 2nd Battalion the Parachute Regiment [2 Para] fought an epic battle at the main road bridge).

***Generalfeldmarschall* Rommel and his staff on a tour of inspection north of Bruneval, 1944.**

Major John Frost became 2IC of 2 Para. When the CO (Lieutenant Colonel G P Gofton-Salmond) fell ill just before sailing for North Africa, he took command and led it in Tunisia,

Sergeant (then Corporal) Gregor McKenzie with a group of C Company soldiers in Devizes in January 1942. Back row (from the left) - Privates Judge, Conroy, McCann, Herwood and Higgins. Front row - Lance Corporal Fleming, Corporal McKenzie, Sgt Muir and Private O'Neill.

Sicily, Italy and at Arnhem where he was taken prisoner. Frost was awarded the DSO and Bar while in command of 2 Para. Having been freed by US troops in March 1945, he resumed command and took 2 Para to Palestine. He went on to serve in the Malayan Emergency, commanded 52nd (Lowland) Infantry Division and was General Officer Commanding Malta and Libya before retiring as a Major General in 1968.

Distinguished Conduct Medal.

In North Africa, Sergeant Gregor McKenzie added the Distinguished Conduct Medal to the Military Medal awarded for Bruneval. He was captured in December 1942 and held at Capua in Italy, from where he made a successful escape.

Captain John Ross was awarded the DSO for his service in North Africa in late 1942. Frost gave him command of C Company aged only twenty-one and he took it into Sicily in July 1943. He was dropped in the wrong place and taken prisoner. For his activities on the escape committee in captivity he was awarded the MBE. After service in the Far East until 1947, he practiced law in Dundee, served in the Territorial Army and was a Deputy Lieutenant for Tayside.

Member of the British Empire.

CSM Strachan was on the danger list for some time after Bruneval, but recovered and rejoined the Battalion to become the Regimental Sergeant Major. He was wounded again and taken prisoner at Arnhem, but died in Sheffield in 1948 after an operation brought on by complications with the wounds sustained at Bruneval.

John Timothy became liaison officer with the first American airborne unit in Britain and was the first British parachutist to be awarded American jump wings. He jumped into action with US forces in North Africa before rejoining 2 Para in January 1943. On 8 March 1943, with his platoon surrounded and under heavy fire, he went out and captured two machine guns having killed six enemy gunners, for which he was awarded the MC. He missed the Sicily landings due to illness, but was dropped behind enemy lines in Italy in October 1943 on a search and rescue mission for escaped allied POWs (Operation SIMCOL), for which he was awarded a Bar to his MC. He took R Company of 1 Para into Arnhem and was awarded a second Bar to his MC for a determined attack towards the road bridge before being taken prisoner. When the Germans shifted the inmates of *Oflag VIIB* in Bavaria westwards away from the advancing Russians, he escaped and met up with advancing US Forces. Timothy returned to Marks & Spencer for the rest of his working career. He was military adviser for the film *School for Secrets*, produced and directed by Peter Ustinov.

By an ironic twist Philip Teichman became Frost's 2IC, although he was senior to him. He was killed in North Africa in December 1942. His father endowed four scholarships at Caius College and one at Inner Temple in memory of his sons Philip and Major Dennis Patrick Teichman MC killed in Normandy in 1944.

Cook returned home in September 1942 when the Australian government asked for advice in setting up a Combined Operations Training Centre. He established the Amphibious Training Centre at Port Stephens as HMAS *Assault*.

Sir Henry Nigel Norman went on to be air commander for the North African landings. He was killed on 19 May 1943 when the aircraft taking him to North Africa force-landed after taking off from RAF St Mawgan in Cornwall.

Charles Pickard was the first RAF officer in the war to be awarded the DSO and two Bars. He flew numerous covert sorties in Lysanders from Tempsford, dropping supplies and SOE agents into occupied Europe. Commanding 140 Wing he led the 18 February 1944 low-level attack on Amiens Prison (Operation JERICHO). The operation was a success, but Pickard and his navigator, Flight Lieutenant Bill Broadley DSO DFC DFM (also his navigator at Bruneval), were killed when their Mosquito was shot down by a Fw 190 flown by *Feldwebel* Mayer of *7 Jagdgeschwader 26*. They are buried in St Pierre Cemetery near Amiens.

R V Jones was involved in numerous other scientific intelligence projects and became a V1/V2 expert on the Cabinet Defence Committee (Operations). In 1946 he left Government service, unhappy with the post war organisation of scientific intelligence, and became Chair of Natural Philosophy at the University of Aberdeen. At Churchill's request, in 1952, he became Director of Scientific Intelligence at the Ministry of Defence, but resumed his academic duties in Aberdeen at the end of 1953, remaining there until retirement in 1981. Amongst the many national and international honours bestowed upon him, in 1993 he was the first recipient of the R V Jones

Intelligence Award, created by the US Central Intelligence Agency. A full description of his war work appeared in his book, *Most Secret War* in 1978.

Browning is famous for coining the phrase, 'a bridge too far' about the Market-Garden operation in September 1944, during which he commanded I Airborne Corps. In December 1944 he became Chief of Staff to Mountbatten in South East Asia Command. Following retirement in January 1948 he became Comptroller and Treasurer to Princess Elizabeth and, after she ascended in 1952, became Treasurer in the Office of the Duke of Edinburgh. He was Deputy Chairman of the British Olympic Association and Commandant of the British Olympic team in 1948.

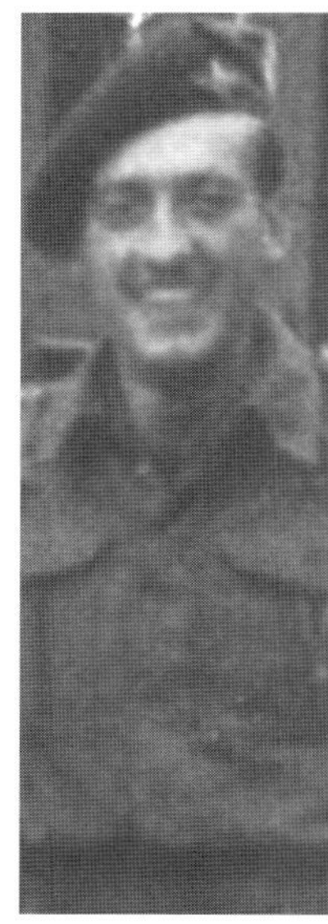
Private Frank McAusland — the only paratrooper in 1st Airborne Division to take part in every one of its operations.

One soldier at Bruneval, Private McAusland, was the only paratrooper in 1st Airborne Division to take part in all its other operations – North Africa, Sicily, Arnhem and the liberation of Norway. After Sicily he transferred to 21st Independent Parachute Company. He was one of those who managed to escape across the Rhine from Oosterbeek perimeter after the failure to seize Arnhem Bridge in September 1944. After the war, from which he emerged without serious injury, he became a stevedore in Liverpool until retiring in 1982. Coincidently, one of his grandchildren was born on a 28 February.

After the war, Cox set up a successful wireless and TV business in Little Church Street in Wisbech. It still exists.

A month after Bruneval, Peter Nagel went on the St Nazaire Raid to support Lieutenant Colonel Charles Newman and was the only British soldier to take part in both operations. To avoid confusion at St Nazaire he reverted to his previous alias of Walker. He was captured, but managed to persuade the Germans, that despite his rather odd accent and continental style tooth fillings, he was actually from Leicester. Held at Marlag und Milag Nord near Bremen, he tried to escape by tunnel, but it was discovered and he was sent to Sandbostel (*Stalag X-B*) for a month, returning briefly to Marlag before being moved to *Stalag VIII-B* at Lamsdorf (now Lambinowice in Poland). From September 1942 he worked in a sugar beet factory then a clothing factory at Jagerndorf (now Krnov in the Czech Republic). As a punishment for being difficult he was sent to a forestry camp in the mountains where he organized minor sabotage. As a result of involvement in a strike, he was returned to Lamsdorf. With a RAF pilot he escaped to Jagerndorf using forged French workers' papers and contacted a Czech girl he had met previously to obtain clothing. They got as far as Klagenfurt in Austria, but were caught and taken to *Gestapo* HQ still pretending to be French workers. They were eventually sent back to Lamsdorf. Nagel was liberated near Munich by the Americans in spring 1945 and returned to Leicester to his father's business, which he took over in the late 1950s. On the 40th anniversary of the Raid he received a *Diplome d'Honneur* signed by Queen Elizabeth II and President François Mitterand.

General Charles de Gaulle unveiled a simple plaque on the roof of the BEACH FORT pillbox 30 March 1947. Twenty thousand former resistance members and deportees attended the ceremony in addition to some of those involved in the raid. De Galle made no mention of the British in his speech and ignored the Parachute Regiment guard of honour. In the narrow confines of the village there was a mix up over traffic arrangements and many guests were forced to walk across country to get there, including the British Ambassador, Duff Cooper and his wife. De Gaulle had lunch at the Hotel Beauminet after the ceremony.

In 1975, massive concrete sea walls were built 300 metres south of Bruneval beach as part of the development of France's second largest oil terminal. Also in 1975 the current memorial was commemorated in the presence of Lord Louis Mountbatten.

The same year, the *After The Battle* magazine team tried to locate the *Würzburg* parts recovered from Bruneval. They could not be traced by the Royal Signals and Radar Establishment at Malvern (successor to TRE), RAE Farnborough or the Imperial War Museum. The Science Museum had some *Würzburg* parts, but their provenance was unclear. More recent investigations concluded the Science Museum *Würzburg* parts, some of which originated in Guernsey, which was not liberated until May 1945, are not from Bruneval. It is also known that the Airborne Forces Museum at Duxford does not have any *Würzburg* parts; 'The last time we saw them was in 1942 when we handed them over to the boffins!' In 1982 the Brenzett Aeronautical Museum had a component, which may have been recovered on the raid, but has been lost subsequently. Inquiries with the Hawkinge Battle of Britain Museum, the Farnborough Air Sciences Trust, The Imperial War Museum and the Purbeck Radar Trust have also failed to locate the Bruneval *Würzburg* components.

Kurt Student, founder of German airborne forces, wrote to Mountbatten in 1976 having seen a Yorkshire TV documentary made to coincide with the anniversary of the raid. He said it sent a great shock through Hitler's HQ. Student was full of admiration.

1982 saw the 40th anniversary of the raid. To mark the occasion a ceremony was held at the memorial in June attended by President François Mitterand. Prince Charles, representing the Queen, was also there in his capacity as Colonel-in-Chief of the Parachute Regiment.

In 1948, Frank Embury was invited to Bruneval, but had recently married and twins were born the same year. There was no opportunity to go back and he lost touch with the French. In 1984 a local newspaper sought him out; Alain Millet was writing a book about the Raid and wanted the soldier's version of events. The leader of the Bruneval/Étretat Resistance, responsible for Embury's planned escape with Cornell, made contact. George Cornell was also contacted and the two were reunited, but Embury died in 1987 before he could return to Bruneval. In 1994, the Royal British Legion contacted his wife Ivy. The Mayor of Bruneval was planning to commemorate the 50th anniversary of the liberation and a plaque was to be dedicated to the two soldiers on the barn where they sheltered at Le Tilleul. Mrs Embury was not in good health, but agreed to go when they said the family would be welcome to attend as well. The ceremony took place on 2 September 1994. The Mayor turned out to be the fifteen-year old farmer's son who discovered Embury and Cornell in the barn that February morning in 1942.

Chapter Twelve

A TOUR OF THE BRUNEVAL BATTLEFIELD

General

A visit to the battlefield can be completed in about half a day. This tour starts near the Cap d'Antifer lighthouse and is divided into seven stands. The area around Bruneval has few facilities

Extract from IGN Série Bleue (1:25,000) Sheet 1710ET showing the location of the seven stands on the tour - the full map is available from www.ign.fr.

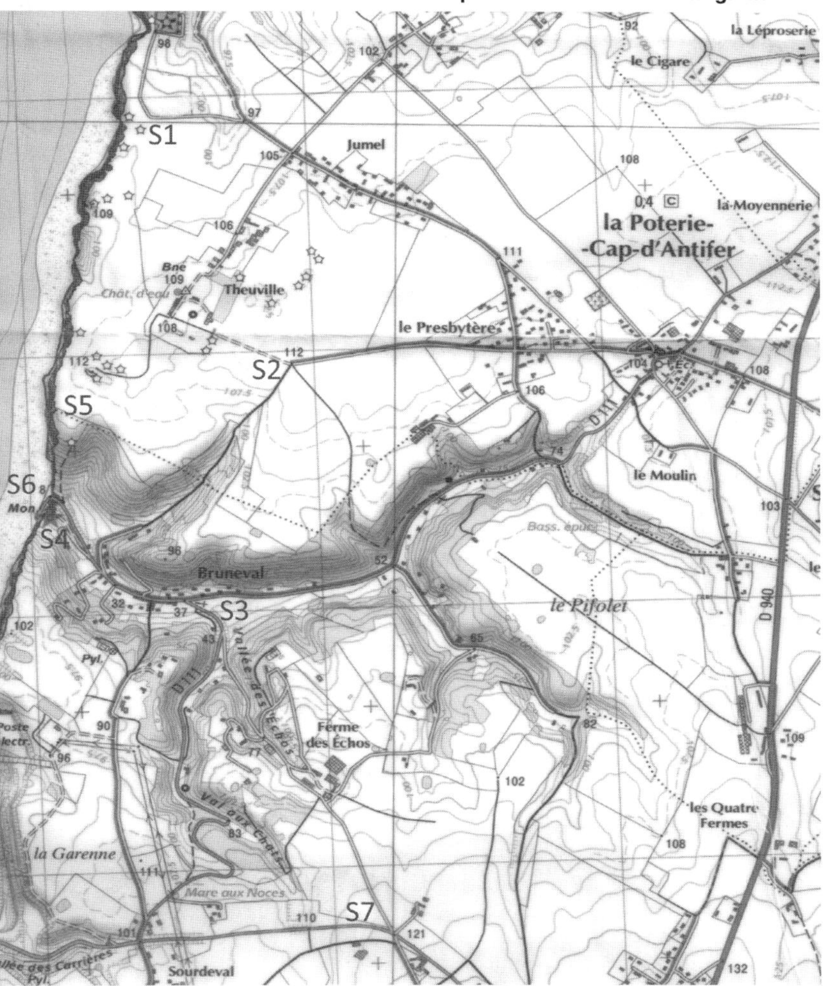

and visitors should go prepared. It can be a windswept and forlorn place in poor weather. Once off the main routes, roads are narrow and some are unpaved. It is not advisable to take large vehicles.

Stand 1 – Anti-Aircraft Gun Battery Cap d'Antifer Lighthouse
The lighthouse is signed off the main Étretat-Le Havre road (D940). Park at the last right hand bend before the lighthouse and walk 50 metres to the first gun position (constructed after the Raid). From the top there are excellent views over the sea, along the cliffs and inland towards Theuville/Le Presbytère (RECTANGLE). A short walk south along the cliff tops (keep away from the unstable edges) brings you to the hexagonal

Base for the *Freya* radar station.

The cliffs near the lighthouse are 105 metres high – beware the unstable edges.

The entrance to Theuville, with the turning area left of the gate.

concrete base of a *Freya* radar station. About 600 metres south of it can be seen the remains of the LONE HOUSE chateau demolished after the raid.

Stand 2 – Track near DZ/RV

Return to your vehicle and start heading back towards the main road. Go straight on at the crossroads at the northwest end of Jumel heading southeast. Pass through the village for 800 metres to a fork in the road and take the right (south) onto Rue des Hortensias in Le Presbytère. After 250 metres at the crossroads go right (west) on Rue du Maj Frost. Stop after 750 metres at a right bend in the main track, where it is joined by two smaller tracks from the left (south). You can turn round here, but in wet

The southern edge of Theuville (RECTANGLE) from the track bend/junction. The remains of the LONE HOUSE chateau are to the left.

From the track bend/junction close to Theuville looking south. On the far hillside, right of the white building, is the area where Charteris' and Grieve's sections landed.

weather it can be difficult. It is easier to go on and turn in the area to the left of the gate into Theuville (RECTANGLE). The property is private and should not be entered, but a reasonable view of the farm complex can be obtained from the gate.

At the track junction there is a good view south along the line of approach of the Whitley jump aircraft. From here you can also see the DZ, RV, RECTANGLE and LONE HOUSE. Look south about two kms and find a prominent white building. Just to the right of it above the wood is the other DZ in a shallow re-entrant.

Stand 3 – Bruneval Village Calvary

Return to the crossroads in Le Presbytère. Go straight on (east) for 400 metres to the centre of La Poterie. Turn right and right again onto the D111, having passed the church on your left. Follow the D111 for just over two kms southwest through a deep wooded re-entrant to the beginning of Bruneval village. Stop at the obvious Calvary road junction in Ave du Col Remy. The Hotel Beauminet was the first house on the left on entering Bruneval at the time of the raid, but there is now another house before it. Charteris' and Grieve's sections both passed close to this point to reach the high ground to the north.

Stand 4 – Memorial

Continue downhill (west) through Bruneval village and the steep sided re-entrant. Turn left up a slope to the memorial and park on the track. Alternatively go on to the small car park just before the beach and use the steps on the south side of the building occupying the site of Stella Maris (GUARD ROOM) to reach the memorial. The memorial is on the remains of BEACH FORT. Looking north from the memorial is the steep slope down which the raiders withdrew. From the cliff edge and steps there are views over the evacuation beach.

The left turn off the beach road to the memorial.

The steps from the car park to the memorial are to the right of the house. They incorporate a stone from Mauthausen concentration camp.

The Bruneval memorial on top of the BEACH FORT pillbox, with the southern cliffs leading t Point 102 beyond.

Captain Ross' section came under fire from th point (BEACH FORT), as it emerged from the tree in the re-entrant top left Ross, Young and Nauomoff later attacked this position from the road, which is hidden in the ravine below.

Sergeant Grieve's section charged towards the camera to seize BEACH FORT, while the others attacked from left of picture out of the ravine.

Stand 5 – Northern Clifftop

This one is not for the faint hearted. Leave the memorial, cross the road in the ravine and climb the well-worn path to the top of the northern cliffs. A concrete pillbox (almost certainly post-raid) is on the site of REDOUBT where the withdrawing raiders came under fire from BEACH FORT and CSM Strachan was seriously wounded. Go on a little further north until reaching a fence to overlook the site of HENRY, LONE HOUSE and RECTANGLE – the fields beyond the fence are private.

Above: From the bottom of the northern cliff path looking inland over the ravine the paratroopers had to cross from left to right in order to seize BEACH FORT

Above: Pillbox at REDOUBT. The DZ is in the distance top left.

Below: From REDOUBT looking north. LONE HOUSE is the hump on the left with RECTANGLE in the right background.

Below: The foundations of LONE HOUSE with one of the post-raid flak positions beyond.

Stand 6 – Beach

Depending on the state of the tide it is possible to gain access to the beach, although this is not recommended and there are signs warning against it. Keep away from the cliffs to avoid loose stones. From the beach you get a feel for the difficulties of finding it and getting off it at night under fire.

Above: These steps can be seen in Tony Hill's side view of the *Würzburg* and on the model of LONE HOUSE. The chateau was to the left and the terrace was on top of the existing cellars to the right. It is sometimes said these are the steps Frost used to enter the front door of the chateau, but the door was well to the left.

t: The low earth bank t surrounded the *rzburg* is circled in the ground with the ains of LONE HOUSE ind. The concrete ucture in the left tance is the base for a r *Wassermann* radar.

Above: A German barbed wire picket still in service on the cliffs above Bruneval.

Stand 7 – Other DZ

Return to the Calvary and turn right on the D111 for 1.8 kms. Turn left at a major junction into Rue des Pruniers. After 700 metres stop at a Y junction on the left to overlook the DZ at the head of Val aux Chats. RECTANGLE is clearly visible in the distance to the north.

If time permits the barn where Privates Embury and Cornell sheltered may be viewed in Le Tilleul. From Stand 7 return to the main D940 road and head north towards Étretat. On entering the village of Le Tilleul turn right at the church past the hotel. Go east for 375m, turn right for 120m and stop at the T-junction. The barn with a memorial on the roadside wall is across the road.

FACILITIES

In the immediate area of the battlefield there are none, but a little further afield are the following (distances are approximated from the memorial):

St Jouin-Bruneval (three and a half kilometres) – a tiny bar/tabac on the main street and a bakers.

Belvedere Restaurant (three kilometres) – on the cliffs between Bruneval and St Jouin-Bruneval. It is pricey and only opens for lunch and dinner in the season.

Le Tilleul – there is parking for about eight cars in the centre. The restaurant is not a café (open 1200-1400 & 1900-2100 daily (2130 Fri & Sat), closed Mon-Tue). The hotel has a small bar, which serves coffee. The bakers opens 0700-1300 & 1400-1900, but is closed Tue and Sun afternoon.

Étretat – is a lovely old seaside town with many restaurants and bars etc, but it is very busy in high season. There are plenty of pay car parks so have some change available, and be aware that some involve a fairly long walk into the centre. In the central car park is the Café/Bar le Weekend near the Mairie (open Mon 0900-1300 & 1500-1900, Tue-Fri 0730-2000, Sat-Sun 0800-2000).

Claude Monet painted the spectacular cliffs at Étretat in the 1880s and 90s.

Appendix I

BATTLE OF THE BEAMS

Early in 1940, Dr R V Jones became convinced the Germans had a system of electronic beams to facilitate accurate night bombing. In fact the Germans used three systems, namely *Knickebein*, *X-Gerät* and *Y-Gerät*, which Jones and others managed to counter and thereby put scientific intelligence on the map.

Knickebein **(CROOKED LEG)**

Knickebein was based upon *Lorenz* blind landing equipment, introduced by *Lufthansa* in 1934 and in use throughout the world by the outbreak of war. Two collocated transmitters, one producing dots and the other dashes were aimed over the target. Where the two transmissions met, the dashes and dots merged to produce a continuous signal. Bombers flew down the continuous signal until they crossed a second similar beam and released their bombs.

Prisoners revealed *Knickebein* was accurate to less than 1,000 metres and one said it was as accurate as *X-Gerät*, taking it for granted the British were conversant with both; they were not, until then that is. Units equipped with *Knickebein* appeared to be in *Flieger Korps IV*, so Jones hunted for unusual equipment in its crashed aircraft. A prisoner chatting privately revealed that no matter how hard they looked, the British would not find the equipment; it therefore had to be something obvious. The only item that fitted the bill was the *Lorenz* blind landing receiver. The man who evaluated the equipment at Farnborough told Jones there was nothing unusual about it, except it was much more sensitive than required for blind landing. Another prisoner confirmed *Knickebein* was a bombing device based upon intersecting radio beams and drew a picture of the transmitter towers. The picture matched an antenna photographed near Sylt where there was a *Lorenz* beacon; Jones had cracked it.

Churchill's scientific adviser, Professor Frederick Lindemann, alerted the Prime Minister to the danger and a committee of inquiry was formed. Jones set up receivers at five Chain Home stations to detect the beams as they were switched on and establish which stations they were passing between. Then an

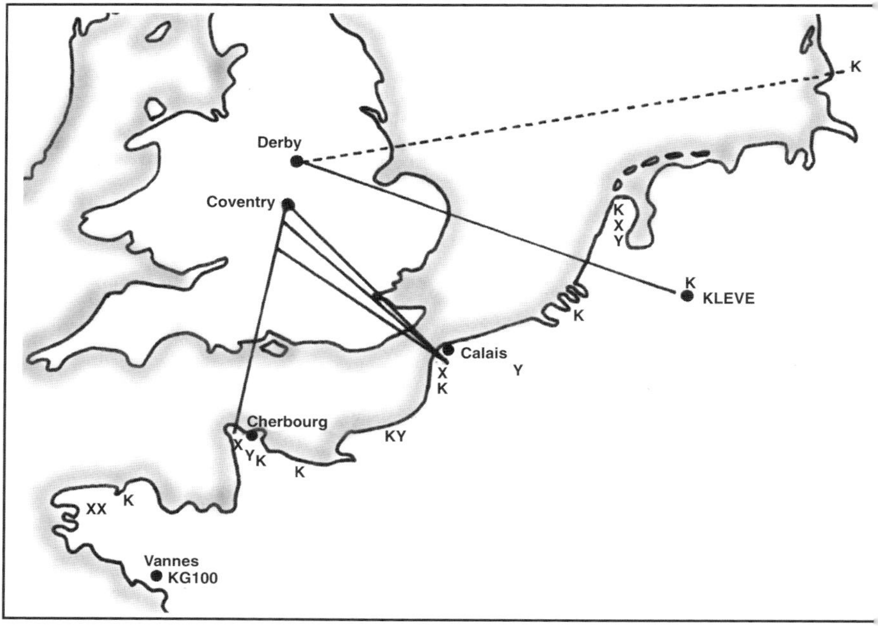

Location of the beam ground stations – ***Knickebein*** **(K), X-*Gerät* (X) and Y-*Gerät* (Y). The *Knickebein* beam from Kleve is shown set up for a raid on Derby with the cross beam transmitted from Schleswig-Holstein close to the Danish border. *X-Gerät* is shown configured for the raid on Coventry on 14 November 1940 with the main beam transmitted from Cherbourg and the three cross beams from Calais.**

Anson, fitted with receivers and flown by an experienced *Lorenz* trained pilot from the Blind Approach Development Unit at Boscombe Down, was tasked to plot it accurately. On 21 June an Anson flying between Huntingdon and Lincoln picked up clear dot signals. After flying on for a few minutes these merged to form a continuous note, which later broke up into a series of dashes.

Avro Anson.

Crude jammers, improvised from hospital cauterizing equipment, were set up in police stations all over the country to be switched on by request. *Lorenz* transmitters were also used to distort the beams and reduce their accuracy. Jamming beacons, known as Meacons, were sited strategically and set daily to the

Luftwaffe frequencies to make life complicated for German navigators. A little later a bespoke *Knickebein* jammer named Aspirin was developed, so called because *Knickebein* was known as Headache. Aspirin only sent out dashes, but it was enough to send bombers off course, or to fly in circles; *Knickebein* had been rendered ineffective.

X-Gerät

X-Gerät (apparatus) was first used in the bombing of Warsaw in 1939. The system used against Britain consisted of a main beam (*Weser*), transmitted from Cherbourg, with a number of crossing beams, transmitted from Calais (*Rhine, Oder, Elbe*). Bombers flew along *Weser*, which was laid over the target. When they crossed *Rhine* it alerted the crews they were nearing the target. When they crossed *Oder* the bomb aimers started both hands on a special clock sweeping in the same direction. As they crossed *Elbe* the first hand stopped and the second hand reversed. The next time the hands overlapped the bombs were released.

Jones was alerted to *X-Gerät* by a conversation recorded between two *Luftwaffe* prisoners. Early in September intelligence revealed it was accurate to 200 metres over 300 kms and was fitted to aircraft with the call sign *6N + LK*. It was known that the unit using that call sign was *Kampfgeschwader 100* (*KG 100*), based at Vannes in northwest France. The frequencies to be used each night were transmitted in the afternoon. Provided the signal was intercepted and decoded in time, 80 Wing RAF would be able to jam them and night fighters could be positioned to attack the incoming bombers.

TRE devised a jammer named Bromide. On 5 November 1940, *KG 100* was involved in a raid on Birmingham. One aircraft was hopelessly disorientated by a Meacon and, almost out of fuel, landed just off Chesil Beach in Dorset. The *X-Gerät* receivers were rushed to Farnborough. Examination revealed they worked on five frequencies, with three more on stand-by to evade jamming. These eight frequencies were chosen daily from the twenty that the system could use. To be effective the jammers had to know these frequencies beforehand.

Intercepted signals revealed a German plan to destroy three industrial cities in mid-November; the targets were Wolverhampton, Birmingham and Coventry, but the order in which they were to be attacked was not known. On 14

Radio operator of a Ju88 tuning-in his equipment.

November it was clear a raid was developing and it was suspected that the target was in the Midlands. The jammers wanted to know the frequencies and Jones did not have sufficient information to be accurate, so he made an educated guess. The *KG 100* aircraft at first flew well outside *Weser* to avoid night fighters, edging closer to the beam as they neared the target. They heard a lot of interference, but could just make out the real signals. The incendiaries were released automatically and the bomber squadrons flew in to release their bombs over the resultant fires; Coventry was devastated.

Jones had made an accurate guess about the frequencies, but someone had set the audible tone on the jammers at 1,500 cycles rather than 2,000, which meant the German crews could just hear the correct signal. With the audible signal problem fixed, the attack on Birmingham failed as most bombs fell well outside the city. The *Luftwaffe* cancelled the raid on Wolverhampton; *X-Gerät* had been mastered.

Y-Gerät

This system used a single beam, along which the bomber flew. Pulses were transmitted from the ground station to the bomber, which returned them until the correct time lapse indicated it was time to drop the bombs.

On 27 June 1940 an Ultra intercept revealed, 'It is proposed to set up *Knickebein* and *Wotan* installations near Cherbourg and Brest.' Jones knew about *Knickebein* and read that *Wotan* was a one-eyed Teutonic god. Knowing how obvious the Germans could be, he deduced the system operated on a single beam. On 6 October another Ultra intercept gave coordinates for the Royal Armoured Corps Depot at Bovington, but no directions, reinforcing the theory that a single station was able to direct the bombers. Bovington was attacked a few nights later, not very accurately for direction, but spot on for range.

Alexandra Palace and the television transmitter tower. The fledgling BBC television service was suspended during the war, allowing the transmitter to be used as a jammer against *Y-Gerät*.

Analysis of the beam revealed left and right signals with a pause between each. To maintain accurate direction the pilot kept between the two using a visual indicator. The British simply picked up the aircraft's return signal and reradiated it back to the aircraft, which the aircraft radiated again. The effect was like feedback on a microphone and resulted in false distance calculations. The first jammer, Domino, began operating from Highgate in London in February 1941 and soon after a second was in use on Beacon Hill, near Bulford on Salisbury Plain. At full power, the BBC television transmitter at Alexandra Palace cancelled out the *Y-Gerät* system. In an attempt to avoid these countermeasures, the Germans set up new ground stations and changed frequencies, but they could not win a power output battle over Britain. Soon after the *Luftwaffe* was diverted to Russia and the battle of the beams over Britain was over.

Beacon Hill on the edge of Salisbury Plain alongside the A303. This is where the second Domino jammer was set up by 80 Wing. It was so successful, the Luftwaffe bombed the site on 11 and 13 March 1941, but without disrupting its operations.

Appendix II

PHOTOGRAPHIC RECONNAISSANCE UNIT

During the First World War an Australian, Sidney Cotton, was a pilot in the Royal Naval Air Service. As a result of suffering freezing temperatures in the air, he designed the one-piece 'Sidcot' flying suit to keep warm; it was in service with the RAF until the 1950s. Cotton was apt to flout authority and as a result of one incident resigned his commission in October 1917.

Between the wars he was involved in all sorts of schemes on the ground and in the air, including

Left: Frederick Sidney Cotton in 1941.

The three pilots standing are wearing Sidcot suits in this late First World War picture.

Sidney Cotton's Lockheed 12A.

developing high quality air photographs. Just before the Second World War, Wing Commander Fred Winterbotham of MI6 approached Cotton. A private aircraft was needed to take clandestine aerial photographs of the German military buildup. Cotton agreed to help and a Lockheed 12A was bought. Using his cover as a wealthy private aviator promoting his film business and other subterfuges, he undertook a series of flights and provided valuable information about German military and naval activity.

However, Cotton had a poor experience flying with the French military intelligence agency, the Deuxieme Bureau, and turned over the Lockheed to them. He ordered another, which arrived in May 1939. Three RAF F24 cameras were mounted; two looking sideways and one straight down to cover a greater area, plus a Leica in each wing. Sliding panels made them practically invisible. The aircraft was painted duck-egg green to make it difficult to see. With Canadian Bob Niven, he flew to Malta and carried out a mission with RAF pilot Shorty Longbottom. Cotton and Niven then covered parts of Sicily, the eastern Mediterranean, North Africa and Ethiopia.

RAF F24 aerial photography cameras fitted to a Spitfire.

Cotton's business making Dufaycolor film interested the Germans and he arrived at Tempelhof Airport, Berlin on 26th July 1939. He managed to fix a flight with *Luftwaffe* General Albert Kesselring aboard. With Kesselring at the controls, Cotton reached under his seat to operate the cameras as they flew over the airfield. With Germany about to invade Poland he was recalled. Despite delays Cotton and Niven were allowed to take off for England on a prescribed route, but it didn't stop them photographing the German fleet in Schilling Roads on the way.

At a meeting in London, Cotton was asked for advice on RAF camera problems as he produced better pictures. Cotton achieved this using the same cameras, but played warm air over them to stop condensation freezing and used better quality film and development processes. At the same meeting it was mentioned that pictures were needed of two Dutch ports. Cotton volunteered, but the RAF officials baulked at a civilian flying a military mission. They decided to meet next day with a RAF expert who would disprove Cotton's claims about the cameras.

Cotton rang Niven at Heston to get the Lockheed ready. An hour later they took off, ostensibly for a test off the Kent coast, flew over both Dutch ports and landed at Farnborough. The photographic section worked all night and Cotton attended the meeting next day with senior RAF officers and experts. Cotton withstood the skepticism for half an hour and then slapped the pictures on the table. The others were impressed, but declared such quality could not be expected in wartime. Cotton told them they were taken the previous afternoon and walked out, leaving the meeting in uproar. Next day he was offered command of the RAF's photographic section.

On 24 September, Cotton set up the Heston Flight when the RAF took over his company. Men (including Niven and Longbottom), equipment and facilities were made available. Cotton demanded and received Spitfires, which he stripped out, polished and tuned to increase speed. The unit became known as 'Cotton's Club' or 'Cotton's Crooks' because they repeatedly flouted regulations. As a result Cotton designed a special badge, 'CC-11', standing for Cotton's Crooks plus the 11th Commandment – thou shalt not be found out!

The Flight was renamed a number of times; in November 1939 it was No.2 Camouflage Unit, in January 1940 it became the

The PRU Spitfire memorial at RAF Benson – the sideways looking camera aperture is between the rear of the cockpit and the roundel.

Photographic Development Unit, by June 1940 it was the Photographic Reconnaissance Unit (PRU) and in November 1940 it became No.1 Photographic Reconnaissance Unit before expanding into five separate squadrons. The unit was equipped with a variety of modified aircraft, including Blenheims, Hudsons, Spitfires and later Mosquitoes.

Cotton had many successes, but had a habit of embarrassing the establishment. He clashed with the Air Ministry for participating in the evacuation of British agents from France under cover of special survey flights. After picking up the head of Christian Dior for a fee, he was removed from post on 16 June 1940. Following unsuccessful efforts to be reinstated he resigned his commission, but was awarded the OBE and acted as an unofficial adviser throughout the war. Without Cotton, the Bruneval *Würzburg* radar may not have been detected.

Appendix III

KAMMHUBER LINE

Majorgeneral Josef Kammhuber's air defence line covered the western borders of the Reich and was known to the Germans as the Himmelbett (four poster bed) Line. It stretched from Denmark to the middle of France, lying across the route British bombers had to take to attack targets in Germany. The Line consisted of a series of 'boxes' each with a frontage of twenty kilometres, a depth of thirty-two kilometres and height equating to the ceiling of the incoming bombers, about six kilometres; thus giving the schematic appearance of a four poster bed. Within each box was a primary and backup night-fighter. A *Freya* radar directed a master searchlight onto a target and other searchlights in range followed its lead, allowing flak units and the night-fighter to engage it.

As the bomber offensive grew in intensity many searchlights were withdrawn from the Himmelbett Line for the point defence of the main cities. Later each box was provided with two *Würzburg* radars, one to track the night fighter and the other to

***Majorgeneral* Josef Kammhuber – he fought throughout the First World War and remained in the tiny post-war army. In 1930 he trained as a pilot in the USSR and then joined the staff of the *Luftwaffe* Chief of Staff (COS). Disillusioned with unrealistic expansion programmes, he requested an active duty post and became COS of *Luftlotte 2*. He and his commander were sacked by Hitler following the Mechelen Incident, when a liaison plane carrying plans for the forthcoming invasion of France and the Low Countries crash landed in Belgium in January 1940. Kammhuber then commanded a bomber unit and was shot down and held prisoner until released after the Battle of France in July 1940. His next position was to coordinate flak, searchlight and radar units, which resulted in the Himmelbett Line. Following disagreements over the selection of new night-fighters he was transferred to Norway, where he spent most of the rest of the war. Released by the Allies in 1948, he worked for the US Department of Defense and served in the reformed *Luftwaffe* 1956-1962.**

lock onto a target. Radar operators sent frequent position reports to the box control centre, where controllers directed the night-fighter close enough to the target for visual interception.

In February 1942 an object sounding like a *Freya* was reported five kms north of the German night-fighter base at St Trond in Belgium. Subsequent photographs showed the *Freya* and two *Würzburg Riese*, plus three searchlights. The British relied upon a single radar to track target and interceptor on a Plan Position Indicator (PPI), forerunner of modern air traffic control systems. British radar experts expected the Germans to use the same system. However, Dr R V Jones believed the two *Würzburg* were located side by side to track the target and interceptor separately, with the two tracks being fused for the fighter controller. Jones was correct.

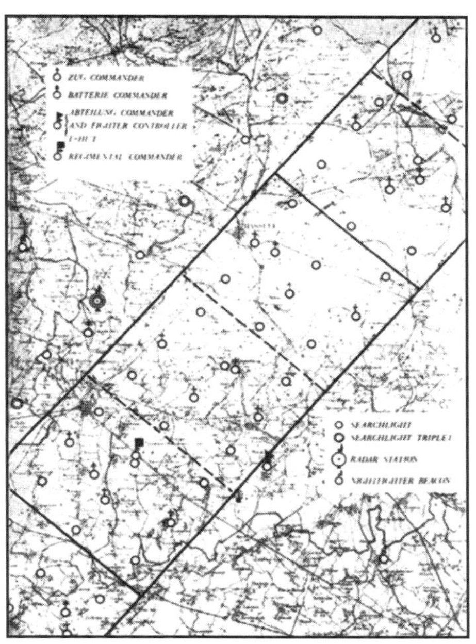

A map of one section of the Himmelbett Line retrieved by a resistance agent in April 1942.

When *Lichtenstein* airborne interception radar was fitted to German night-fighters, it allowed pilots to seek out the target

Lichtenstein **airborne interception radar fitted to a Messerschmitt Bf 110 G-4 night-fighter.**

themselves, once ground controllers had directed them into the general area. This development made the remaining searchlights redundant and, with minor variations, this was the format of the Himmelbett Line for the rest of the war.

Appendix IV

SOURCES

By Air to Battle. HMSO 1945.
Combined Operations 1940-42. HMSO 1943.
The Red Beret. Hilary St George Saunders 1950.
Wings of Night; The Secret Missions of Group Captain Pickard DSO and two Bars DFC. Alexander Hamilton 1977.
Operation Biting; The Naval Story of the Bruneval Raid 27/28 February 1942. Capt Frederick Cook DSC RAN in the *Naval Historical Journal of Australia* 1997.
Wings Of War: Airborne Warfare 1918-1945. Peter Harclerode 2005.
History of the Second World War: The Defence of the United Kingdom. Basil Collier 1957.
Without Tradition; 2 Para 1941-1945. Robert Peatling 1994.
A Drop Too Many. John Frost 1980.
The Bruneval Raid; Stealing Hitler's Radar. George Millar 1974.
Most Secret War: British Scientific Intelligence, 1939-1945. R V Jones 1978.
Bruneval Raid: Operation Biting 1942. Ken Ford 2010.
Commando Country. Stuart Allan, National Museums Scotland 2007.
National Archives:
  BITING and Bruneval files in ADM, AIR, DEFE and WO – including the accounts of individuals involved.
  Peter Nagel papers in HO 396/64/044 and HS 9/1084/2.
Paradata website
Airborne Forces Museum archive.

Appendix V

PARACHUTE FORCE NOMINAL ROLL

There are two versions of the aircraft manifests for the operation, plus another for the 15 February practice jump. The operational manifests appear in the National Archives under AIR 2/7689 and WO 166/6547. Another version appears in "Without Tradition – 2 Para 1941-1945" by Robert Peatling. The two versions differ in the order of jumping, but with one exception the names agree. The exception is in the NELSON aircraft flown by Wing Commander Pickard. Peatling shows the 8th jumper as Grafton, whereas AIR 2/7689 etc shows Balling. A nominal roll of C Company at Bruneval, held separately by the Airborne Forces Museum archive, agrees with the manifests in all but two cases; it does not include Pte Scott 84, but does include Pte A Young. As a result of these anomalies there are 122 names in the nominal roll, instead of 120.

	Name	Rank	Force	Notes
1	**Addie, W**	Pte	Jellicoe	
2	**Balling**	Pte	Nelson	*Appears in the 15 Feb practice jump and & AIR 2/7689 manifest, but not Peatling's.*
3	**Barnett, F**	Pte	Nelson	*2934817 Cpl Frederick Barnett died 22 Sep 1944. Buried in Arnhem Oosterbeek War Cemetery.*
4	**Beattie, W**	Pte	Drake	
5	**Bennett, C**	Sgt	Rodney	
6	**Bond, J**	Pte	Drake	
7	**Boyd, J**	Sgt	Drake	*Bullet wound in foot.*
8	**Branwhite, C**	Pte	Nelson	
9	**Buchanan, P**	Pte	Rodney	
10	**Burns, W**	LCpl	Jellicoe	*3196639 Sgt William Burns died 18 Sep 1944. Commemorated on the Groesbeek Memorial.*
11	**Cadden, G**	Pte	Rodney	
12	**Calderwood, J**	Pte	Nelson	*Wounded and taken prisoner in North Africa. Escaped in Italy but recaptured after 3 months*
13	**Campbell**	Cpl	Rodney	
14	**Charteris, E B C**	Lt	Nelson	*Died in Tunisia 3 Dec 1942. Buried in Massicault War Cemetery. Son of Brig-Gen John Charteris, Haig's Head of Intelligence on the Western Front.*
15	**Coates, J R**	Pte	Nelson	

16	**Collier, G**	Pte	Rodney	
17	**Conroy, R A**	Pte	Hardy	
18	**Cornell, G**	Pte	Rodney	*One of the signallers left behind with Pte Embury.*
19	**Cox, C W H**	Flt Sgt	Hardy	*RAF radar technician.*
20	**Craw/Graw**	Pte	Rodney	
21	**Creighton, F**	Pte	Nelson	
22	**Crutchley, J G**	Pte	Rodney	
23	**Dickie, H**	LCpl	Nelson	
24	**Dobson, R W**	LCpl	Hardy	*Wounded in Tunisia.*
25	**Draper, R**	Pte	Jellicoe	
26	**Eden, J W**	Pte	Rodney	
27	**Ellis, L**	LSgt	Nelson	*RE.*
28	**Embury, F**	Pte	Rodney	*One of the signallers left behind with Pte Cornell.*
29	**Ewing, A**	Pte	Nelson	*The piper at Tilshead and Thruxton.*
30	**Finlay/Finley, R C**	LCpl	Rodney	
31	**Finney, A E**	Cpl	Rodney	
32	**Flambart**	Pte	Rodney	
33	**Fleming, E**	Sgt	Hardy	
34	**Fleming, J**	Pte	Nelson	
35	**Fleming, W**	LCpl	Rodney	*Awarded MM in North Africa*
36	**Flitcroft, H**	Pte	Jellicoe	
37	**Forsyth, M**	Sgt	Rodney	*CSM Macleod Forsyth was awarded the MM for North Africa 1942-43 and the Soviet Order of the Red Star, one of only 23 awarded to British servicemen.*
38	**Freeman, E D**	Pte	Nelson	*Became a senior magistrate in Nottingham.*
39	**Frost, J D**	Maj	Hardy	*Son of General F D Frost.*
40	**Galey, T**	Pte	Hardy	
41	**Gibbons, A**	Sgt	Nelson	
42	**Gordon, A G**	Pte	Hardy	
43	**Gould**	Pte	Nelson	
44	**Grafton, J R**	Pte	Nelson	*Only appears in Peatling's manifest.*
45	**Grant, W**	Pte	Nelson	*Wounded in abdomen.*
46	**Greenough, T**	Pte	Rodney	
47	**Grieve, D**	Sgt	Nelson	*Killed in North Africa 28 Nov 1942 . Buried in Enfidaville War Cemetery, Tunisia.*
48	**Halliwell, S**	Spr	Hardy	*RE. Taken prisoner at Arnhem.*
49	**Harris, E F**	Spr	Rodney	*RE.*
50	**Hayhurst, J**	Pte	Hardy	
51	**Heard, R**	LCpl	Jellicoe	*RE. Wound in hand.*
52	**Henderson, W Y**	Pte	Nelson	*2889238 Pte William Young Henderson died 14 July 1943. Buried in Catania War Cemetery Sicily.*

53	**Heron, A**	Pte	Nelson	*2818294 Pte Albert Heron died 30 Nov 1942. Commemorated on Medjez-el-Bab Memorial, Tunisia..*
54	**Herwood, M**	Pte	Drake	*4275517 Michael Herwood died 28 Mar 1943. Commemorated on Medjez-el-Bab Memorial, Tunisia.*
55	**Heslop, G**	Cpl	Hardy	*Bullet wound in thigh.*
56	**Higgins, G**	Pte	Rodney	
57	**Hill, T H**	Cpl	Nelson	*Later injured in a training jump, spent the rest of the war guarding POWs.*
58	**Horne, D**	Pte	Nelson	
59	**Hornsby, F W**	Spr	Rodney	*2079370 LCpl Francis William Horsby 1 Para Sqn RE died on 24 Nov 1942. Commemorated on Medjez-el-Bab Memorial, Tunisia.*
60	**Hughes, S A**	Pte	Nelson	*1797700 Pte Sidney Arthur Hughes died 30 Nov 1942. Commemorated on Medjez-el-Bab Memorial, Tunisia.*
61	**Hutchinson, J**	Pte	Rodney	
62	**Johnstone, R T**	LCpl	Rodney	*Taken PoW in Italy, escaped to Switzerland 8 months later and was interned for 14 months.*
63	**Jones, S**	Cpl	Hardy	*RE.*
64	**Judge, J**	Pte	Rodney	
65	**Kerr, J**	LCpl	Nelson	
66	**Keyes, H**	Pte	Hardy	
67	**Laughland, T**	Pte	Nelson	
68	**Lough, E**	Pte	Rodney	
69	**Lumb, T**	Sgt	Rodney	
70	**Lutener, N**	Sgt	Drake	
71	**MacCallum, J**	LCpl	Rodney	*Left behind.*
72	**MacFarlane, W**	Sgt	Hardy	*3053379 Sgt William MacFarlane died 30 Nov 1942. Commemorated on Medjez-el-Bab Memorial, Tunisia.*
73	**Manning, N T**	Spr	Jellicoe	*1879829 Spr Norman Thomas Manning 1 Para Sqn RE died 24 Nov 1942. Commemorated on Medjez-el-Bab Memorial, Tunisia.*
74	**Matkin, H C**	Pte	Nelson	*2934514 Pte Henry Charles Matkin died in North Africa 1 Dec 1942 aged 24. Commemorated on Medjez-el-Bab Memorial, Tunisia.*
75	**McAusland, F**	Pte	Jellicoe	*The only paratrooper in 1st Airborne Division to take part in all its operations – Bruneval, North Africa, Sicily, Arnhem and the liberation of Norway.*
76	**McCann, H**	Pte	Rodney	

77	**McCormack, P**	Pte	Nelson	
78	**McIntyre, H D M**	Rfn	Hardy	*3252284 Rfn Hugh Duncan McDonald* McIntyre *killed at Bruneval 28 Feb 1942. Buried at Ste Marie Cemetery, Le Havre, France alongside Pte Scott.*
79	**McKenzie, G**	Sgt	Jellicoe	*Previous service in Black Watch. Deerstalker and later postman. Rejoined Jun 1940. DCM MM.*
80	**McLennon, W**	Cpl	Nelson	*Taken PoW in North Africa, escaped in Italy and faught with partisans before rejoining British Forces*
81	**McLeod, J**	Pte	Hardy	
82	**Millington, J**	Pte	Rodney	
83	**Mitchell, V J**	Spr	Nelson	*2074436 Spr Victor John Mitchell died 24 Nov 1942. Commemorated on Medjez-el-Bab Memorial, Tunisia.*
84	**Muir, R**	Sgt	Rodney	
85	**Murphy, F O B**	Pte	Drake	
86	**Naoumoff, P**	Lt	Drake	*B Coy, then Battalion Intelligence Officer. Late addition to the raiding force, he does not appear on the manifest for the practice drop 15 Feb.*
87	**Newman/Nagel, P**	Pte	Hardy	*Trained at SOE Special Training Schools, proving to be clear thinking, quick to grasp instructions and make plans. He was enthusiastic, reliable and courageous, but impetuous and not rated as a leader.*
88	**O'Neill, P J**	Pte	Rodney	
89	**Reid, J**	Sgt	Rodney	
90	**Richardson, C**	Pte	Rodney	
91	**Ross, J G**	Capt	Nelson	
92	**Scott, A W**	Pte	Rodney	*5347681 Pte Alan Whorton Scott, Royal Berkshire Regt killed at Bruneval 28 Feb 1942. Buried at Ste Marie Cemetery, Le Havre alongside Rfn McIntyre.*
93	**Scott 335, R I**	Pte	Rodney	*Presented a Fairburn-Sykes knife to 51 Sqn RAF.*
94	**Scott 84**	Pte	Hardy	*2929484 Cpl Richard Robert Scott killed in North Africa 30 Nov–4 Dec 1942. Commemorated on Medjez-el-Bab Memorial, Tunisia.*
95	**Sharp, J L.**	Sgt	Nelson	*Awarded MM for actions in France 1940 and a Bar for North Africa 1942-1943.*

96	**Shaw, H**	Pte	Nelson	*Wounded in leg, compound fractures of tibia and fibula. Wounded and taken prisoner at Arnhem.*
97	**Stacey, G E**	Pte	Rodney	
98	**Stephenson, C**	Pte	Rodney	
99	**Stewart, V**	Cpl	Nelson	*Wounded in scalp.*
100	**Stirling, R**	Pte	Rodney	
101	**Strachan, G A**	CSM	Hardy	*Wounded in abdomen and again at Arnhem. Died in 1948 after an operation on wounds.*
102	**Sturgess, W**	Pte	Nelson	
103	**Sunley, W**	Sgt	Nelson	
104	**Sutherland, J**	Pte	Nelson	*Badly wounded and had to be left behind.*
105	**Synyer, A**	Pte	Nelson	
106	**Tasker, J P**	Sgt	Nelson	
107	**Taylor, G W**	Pte	Hardy	
108	**Thacker, G E**	Pte	Nelson	
109	**Thomas, D**	Pte	Rodney	*Left behind.*
110	**Timothy, J**	Lt	Rodney	
111	**Venters, P L**	Pte	Nelson	
112	**Vernon, D**	Lt	Hardy	*RE. Took part in Tunisian campaign and commanded 2 Para Sqn in Italy.*
113	**Walker, J**	Cpl	Rodney	
114	**Ward, A**	Pte	Rodney	*Taken PoW North Africa. Escaped dressed as a German soldier but was recaptured.*
115	**Webster, A S**	LCpl	Drake	*Wounded in North Africa.*
116	**Welch, F**	Pte	Drake	
117	**Williamson F**	Pte	Drake	*Later DCM and MM. Taken PoW in North Africa and escaped twice. Joined 6th AB Div for Rhine crossing Mar 1945 and was wounded.*
118	**Willoughby, J**	Pte	Nelson	*Left behind.*
119	**Wilson, J**	Pte	Jellicoe	
120	**Wood, F**	Pte	Hardy	
121	**Young, A**	Pte	Hardy	*Only appears on 15 Feb practice drop manifest and AB Forces Museum nominal roll. Claimed he was in Sgt Grieve's Nelson section.*
122	**Young, P A**	Lt	Jellicoe	*R Coy, attached to C Coy for Bruneval only. Not to be confused with the Commando Peter Young.*

Appendix VI

USEFUL INFORMATION

ACCOMMODATION – there is a wide variety of accommodation available between Le Havre (20 kms) ar Étretat (7 kms). For hotels in the area see – www.france-voyage.com/hotels-guide/search.php?kw=Sain Jouin-Bruneval. There is a campsite, Le Grand Hameau, 1.5 kms south of St Jouin-Bruneval on the D11 For B&B accommodation in the area see the local commune website – www.st-jouin-bruneval.fr/.

CLOTHING AND KIT – even in summer it may be cool on the coast. Consider taking: Waterproofs. Headwe and gloves. Walking shoes/boots. Shades and sunscreen. Binoculars and camera. Snacks and drinks.

CUSTOMS/BEHAVIOUR – local people are tolerant of battlefield visitors but please respect their property an address others respectfully – Monsieur, Madame or Mademoiselle. It is rude not to give a general greetin when entering a shop, "Bonjour Messieurs Dames". The French are less inclined to switch to English tha other Europeans. If you try some basic French it will be appreciated.

DRIVING IN FRANCE – rules of the road are similar to UK, apart from having to drive on the right of cours If in doubt about priorities, give way to the right (serrez à droite). The minimum age to drive is 18 with full driving licence. Obey laws and road signs – police impose harsh on-the-spot fines. Penalties f drinking and driving are heavyand the legal limit is lower than UK (50mg rather than 80mg). Stop sigr mean it.

Fuel – petrol stations are only open 24 hours on major routes. Some accept credit cards in automati tellers. The cheapest fuel is at hypermarkets.

Mandatory Requirements – if taking your own car you need:
Full driving licence.
Vehicle registration document.
Comprehensive motor insurance valid in France (Green Card).
European breakdown and recovery cover.
Letter of authorisation from the owner if the vehicle is not yours.
Spare set of bulbs, headlight beam adjusters, warning triangle, GB sticker, high visibility vest an breathalyzer (mandatory sometime in 2012).

Emergency Details – keep details required in an emergency separate from your wallet or handbag:
Photocopy passport, insurance documents and EHIC (see Health below).
Mobile phone details.
Credit/debit card numbers and cancellation telephone contacts.
Travel insurance company contact number.

Ferries – the closest ports are Le Havre and Dieppe. Less expensive crossings are to Dunkirk, Calais an Boulogne, but entail a longer drive and, depending upon your chosen route, Autoroute tolls.

HEALTH

European Health Insurance Card – entitles the holder to medical treatment at local rates. Obtaine by forms from Post Offices, online at www.ehic.org.uk/Internet/home.do or call 0845 6062030. Issue free and valid for five years. You are only covered if you have the EHIC with you when you go fo treatment.

Travel Insurance – you are strongly advised to have travel insurance. If you receive treatment get statement by the doctor (feuille de soins) and a receipt to make a claim on return.

Personal Medical Kit – treat minor ailments yourself to save time and money. Pack sufficien prescription medicine for the full trip.

Chemist (Pharmacie) – look for the green cross. They provide some treatment and if unable to hel will direct you to a doctor. Most open 0900-1900 except Sun. Out of hours services (pharmacie d garde) are advertised in Pharmacie windows.

Doctor and Dentist – hotel receptions have details of local practices. Beware privat doctors/hospitals, as extra charges cannot be reclaimed – the French national health service is know as conventionné.

Rabies – contact with infected animals is very rare, but if bitten by any animal, get the woun examined professionally immediately.

APS – produced by Institut Géographique National are available on-line at www.ign.fr or vw.mapsworldwide.com. Série Verte (1:100,000) Sheet 107 gives a general overview of the area and is useful motoring. Série Bleue (1:25,000) Sheet 1710ET covers the Bruneval area in detail.

ONEY

ATMs – at most banks and post offices with instructions in English. Check your card can be used in France and what charges apply. Some banks limit how much can be withdrawn. Let your bank know you will be away, as some block cards if transactions take place unexpectedly.

Banks – generally open 1000-1200 & 1400-1700 weekdays. Some open all day in towns, some close on Mon and some open Sat a.m.

Credit/Debit Cards – major cards are usually accepted, but some have different names – Visa is Carte Bleue and Mastercard is Eurocard.

Exchange – beware 0% commission, as the rate may be poor. The Post Office takes back unused currency at the same rate, which may or may not be advantageous. Since the Euro currency exchange facilities are scarcer.

Local Taxes – if you buy high value items you can reclaim tax. Get the forms completed by the shop, when leaving France have them stamped by Customs, post them to the shop and they will refund about 12%.

SSPORT – a valid passport is required with a few months remaining.

ST – Post Offices (la Poste) open 0800-1700 weekdays and 0800-1200 Sat. Postcard stamps are more readily ailable from vendors, newsagents and tabacs. Postboxes are yellow.

BLIC HOLIDAYS – just about everything closes on public holidays and banks close early the day before. ınsport may be affected, but tourist attractions in high season are unlikely to be. The following dates/days public holidays:

1 January
Easter Monday
1 & 8 May
Ascension Day
Whit Monday
14 July
15 August
1 & 11 November
25 December

ıny businesses and restaurants close for the majority of August.

DIO – If you want to pick up the news from home try:

BBC Radio 4 – 198 kHz long wave.
BBC Five Live – 909 kHz medium wave.
BBC World Service – 648 kHz medium-wave.

OPS – generally open 0900-1200 and 1400-1900 Mon-Sat. In large towns and tourist areas shops tend to open day, some on Sun. Some bakers open Sun a.m. and during the week take later lunch breaks.

LEPHONE

ance to UK – 0044, delete initial 0 then dial the rest of the number.
France – dial the full 10-digit number even if within the same zone.
yphones – cards purchased from post offices, tabacs and newsagents.
obiles – check yours will work in France and the charges.

Emergencies

Ambulance	- 15)
Fire	- 18) 112 from a mobile
Police	- 17)
British Embassy (Paris)	- 01 44 51 31 00

ME ZONE – one hour ahead of UK.

PPING – a small tip is expected by cloakroom and lavatory attendants and porters. Not required in staurants, as a service charge is always included.

OILETS – the best are in museums and the main tourist attractions. Towns usually have public toilets where arkets are held; some are coin operated.

INDEX